THE THAWING MAN

A Heartwarming Journey from Active Addiction to Long-Term Recovery

Derek A. Chowen, RCP

A Two Scotch Funk Publication

DEDICATION

This book is dedicated to my Mom and Dad.

Thanks for everything you two.

I love you.

CONTENTS

ISBN: 978-1-7379154-1-6
Long Cottage Publishing

THE THAWING...

10.01.19

Part of the thawing process that I didn't think to realize is that it continues for as long as you continue to let it.

That is why you are reading the Third* edition of "The Thawing Man."

Since I first published this book in February of 2018, much has been learned. I've since become a Recovery Coach Professional, certified through CCAR (Connecticut Community for Addiction Recovery).

CCAR is the national benchmark for recovery coaching and as of this writing, the RCP designation is held by just over one hundred professionals nationwide.

The trick has been to keep as much of the original content intact, clean it up to make it more mechanically easy to read and add important lessons learned along the way. Hopefully I have achieved all three.

One of my many flaws is my enthusiasm and the condition it causes. I've named it *"enthusiasm blindness"* and there is no little blue pill to counteract its effects. E.B. is what happens when I tear into a new project that I am truly interested or vested in.

Recovery became that project and I was certain that my obsession would be met with equal parts fascination AND understanding by all those around me.

It wasn't.

Another of my other flaws is self-centeredness and it is common among those afflicted with my condition. What I DID discover was that putting down the booze was the easy part.

Finding recovery was where the real work would come in.

Another discovery was that the majority of society and people with substance use disorder have some very similar traits and that many of the lessons I'm learning in recovery can be used by people that have never taken a sip of alcohol or used a drug.

Imagine living life in a more peaceful, thoughtful manner by just changing how you see things. We are all recovering from something. I've been told this book helps one see things differently.

This introduction is going to explain just one of the many things that happens to a person as they begin the journey to recovery and honestly, spiritual well-being. The rest of the book will show you how mightily things change by removing the drug of choice and adding lessons learned along the way.

I was chatting with a friend the other day and we were talking about getting to work on my website. The pictures and data all needed to be backed up so I could work with somewhat reckless abandon. I started the process and saw that over the course of almost two years, I posted 30 blog entries.

That's quite an accomplishment for a guy with Enthusiasm Blindness.

One of the unfortunate side effects of EB is short attention span-itis. Hell out of the gate but not much for stamina - one of my Dad's sayings. Usually I dive into something full bore, figure it out, get bored and quit. This process has been different than anything I've ever experienced. I'm not getting bored.

Over three and a half years of immersion and things continue to get better and remain exciting.

Now I look forward to what's next. It's also the first time I've gone back and looked at the beginning of the process. Wow. Remembering where I was when I started was shocking. Uncomfortable. Dark. I was a mess and trying to show everyone (and myself) how I really wasn't that bad. The pain I was in, coupled with the uncertainty of where I was headed was an incredible strain. Oh, and my coping mechanism of having a drink or ten was no longer available.

The same friend that I was discussing the website with has been a part of this adventure from almost the beginning. She and I were also discussing how raw the writing and emotions were in the beginning of my authoring career. She also made some excellent observations about how the writing smoothed out as I progressed and as I made peace with people and myself.

My Enthusiasm Blindness flared up and I explained the easier readings probably coincided with my thawing out.

She had finally had it with me. "What the heck is thawing out???"

Oops. *EB.*

Expecting others to know exactly what you are talking about simply because you are immersed in the subject is one of the worst side effects of EB. Kind of goes hand in hand with center of the universe-itis. About three weeks "in" (a term for someone in AA seeking recovery), one of the old timers saw some progress but a lot of frustration.
He said, "Take it easy, kid. You are just starting to thaw out." Thaw out? I was? Are you sure? How do you know? What the heck does that mean? "Be patient. Let it come to you. You'll figure it out eventually."

I spent decades drinking to escape. Not just the bad stuff but the good stuff as well. The peaks and valleys were so great that they were hard to deal with. The intensity of a wonderful event was just as draining as one that was horrific.

In the beginning, the effects of my drinking would come and go. I was allowed a reprieve. Years of self-medicating slowly destroyed that reprieve and started to freeze my mind, my body and my spirit.

The years after my wife left sealed my fate. The fire in my soul finally went out. Full blown depression set in and the only thing to do was drink.

Freeze out the feelings. Freeze out the memories. Freeze out the thoughts. Addiction is an insidious disease and it waits for is host to become weak enough to take over. My brain and my heart were frozen solid, floating in alcohol. It quieted the noise and numbed the pain.

It also postponed an inevitable crash to the bottom which you will read about soon enough.

Removing alcohol was just a piece of the thawing process. A

required piece for me but just a piece. The fire in my soul had to be ignited. That wasn't going to happen by reading motivational quotes on social media or listening to people tell me how happy they were about me putting down the bottle.

It was going to take work.

Turns out it was going to take a lot of work but the rewards make the work so worth it. Thawing sounds like such a nice, warming experience. Sitting in the warm summer sun, letting it wash over you, healing you and all the damage that's been done.

Some of it is that warm sunshine. Some of it is not the heat from the sun but the painful, bright sunlight that hurts your eyes.

Thawing is an unintended consequence of recovery and self discovery.

It's been over three and a half years and it's still happening although less drastic now. Here is the takeaway from the intro. You are going to see some ugly stuff. The beginning was rough.

There was more thrashing than thawing. But... It gets better. Everything gets better.
The work is worth it. There is hope. Did I make it on my first try? Nope.
Did I get a peek at what life could be like in recovery if I stuck with it? Yep.
I spent some time writing to those that live with and love those of us in active addiction.
There is plenty of hope to go around.

We do recover.

1 100 LAPS

06.28.16

That's how many times it felt like I drove through the parking lot of the Serenity House, home of the life saving meetings of Alcoholics Anonymous in Charlevoix. It's also how many times I feel like I've tried to start this first chapter.

Unfortunately, that's probably where the parallels stop as I am an incredibly inexperienced writer but I was a very experienced drinker. Now what is the purpose of this book? Why would someone that got "average" grades in creative writing try this?

Because I am going to write a wildly successful book about my journey and hopefully use it to help others avoid or at least pull out of the nose dive that I have experienced so far, silly!
Pretty sure that's what's going to happen. Pretty sure. How long is a chapter supposed to be? Should I be sitting somewhere that Hemingway never did and channel his genius with a pen?

Maybe I just do what one of my best friends said this past Saturday and just write the stuff down. Let it out. Let the ink flow. Get the stuff down on paper. Start telling the story. I'm following that advice tonight with some trepidation and lots of enthusiasm so please hang in there. One hundred laps.

That is a bit of an exaggeration. It was probably only ninety six. Or more likely, three. Why was it so hard to park in one of the many open spaces? The parking lot looked like it belonged in front of a church at happy hour on a Friday! (I'm just guessing that church parking lots are usually empty on a Friday night) Parking wasn't an issue. The weather wasn't an issue. The mean people inside weren't the issue. (They beat you with clubs in those meetings)

Nope, the reason I couldn't stop the car was the nut behind the steering wheel. Walking through that door meant that I was no longer in control. I wasn't in control of alcohol. I wasn't in control of my mind. I wasn't in control of my heart.

I wasn't in control of my soul. It meant that I had to surrender to the fact that I was an alcoholic and that with any luck, I would be in recovery for the rest of my days. Grabbing that door handle meant the chance of being seen walking in to an AA meeting!

Can you imagine!?!

Someone might see me not drinking!

That is the madness that we are afflicted with. I would slide the tires to a screeching halt in front of a pub to get to MY seat, next to MY pals so I could have MY "usual" but I was embarrassed to have someone see me walk through a door that was going to save MY life.

Pretty bright guy, huh? Did I finally find the guts to go in? Yep. Has it been one of the best decisions of my life? Yep. Did the mean people inside beat me with clubs? Nah. Do I like going to those meetings? MY meetings? Absolutely.

That door was the symbol of choice between long term salvation and intense, burning, short term pain. How short term? It's been four months and I am still burning but nothing like the first few weeks.

Recovery isn't for people that need it, it is for people that want it. After four of the fastest, longest months of my life, I want it more than ever.

Thank you for taking a leap of faith and joining me on this journey.

The good stuff is coming, I promise.

2 THE PROCESS

07.06.16

The *"Old Timers"* are the guys you want to be when you grow up. A few have as many years in sobriety as I have living.

Unfortunately that number gets smaller as my years climb and theirs stop. One of the many unique things about this new club I joined is the fee structure because monetarily, there is none.

Nope, the payment plan is to take what you need to get better and give back what you can to help others. That's it. Oh, you can throw a few bucks in the basket as it goes by to cover your cup of coffee but even that isn't required.

The payment to the *Old Timers* is to keep walking through the door, stopping for a coffee, giving a call once in awhile even if it is just to check in and say hello but most of all, show them that you are starting "The Process".
By participating in the meetings, whether it is just showing up and sitting quietly or partaking in the discussions, you are showing them fresh pain.

My experience so far is that seeing that reminder helps the Old

Timers continue The Process as they help the newcomers begin it.
A very fair trade. What is The Process?

The following description is my interpretation and how I work on this condition daily so please bear with me. It is also just a piece of the description so don't worry, this won't be too long. The Process isn't some phrase used by the secret club nor is it something we ask each other after the secret handshake.

"Hey Jim, doing The Process?"
"I'm Processing like a bastard, Tom!"
(These are pretend names of pretend people having a pretend conversation in a pretend meeting so please don't look at your pals named Jim or Tom and think they are alcoholics.)

Nope.

The Process is what we use to achieve and maintain recovery.

Defining it is that easy.

Got it?

One of the most challenging tasks I have attempted. The process is not to be confused with the 12 steps. The 12 steps have been examined to death so I am just going to work on this process thing. How do we start this "Process", you ask?

Simply remove your armor, let your shields down, leave the bunker, any analogy you want to use to describe surrender.

Pretty much do the one thing that most people and all alcoholics are most afraid of. (Snakes are also terrifying but surrender is pretty damn scary, too!)

This is one of the rare instances that surrender is actually victory. Alcoholics are master showmen. We spend our lives refining the art of concealment, or so we think. The longer we practice our craft, the more intricate our armor becomes.

The problem with this theory is that 99% of the time, the only people we are fooling is ourselves. Hard to believe. To start the process, we are forced into humility and acceptance.

Two traits that are not native in the wiring that makes up the alcoholic brain and DEFINITELY not readily available in mine.

At least not at first.
Sitting at a table with incredibly successful people as well as some that haven't achieved quite as much allows one to start realizing that humility and acceptance are not a suggestion, they are a requirement. Alcoholics are problem solvers and more often than not, very bright. Accepting that we can't fix something on our own is not a familiar situation.

Being humble enough to admit we can't fix it and have to ask for help?

No thanks, I'll pass.

That is a generalization of course but not far off. Now picture this: the most arrogant, bullheaded people you know have to admit that they are wrong AND ask other arrogant, bullheaded people for help because they can't fix this ONE THING by themselves.

Can you see why some alcoholics go "back out" even after years of recovery? Have you noticed that I haven't even mentioned booze yet?

I'll leave you with this final thought because I think I am

probably about 5 paragraphs over the definition of a "ramble."

Try to think of a time when you busted your ass to solve a problem that you just KNEW you could solve if you just worked a tiny bit harder.

Maybe your car was running a bit shitty and you almost had it fixed...

Maybe you were working on a website that looked perfect until you published it and something changed...maybe you have been dieting and exercising and just missed that mystical target weight.

Now give up. Stop all the hard work; toss all your effort in the trash and give up.

Admit you can't do it by yourself, you arrogant ass. Now that you are officially a quitter, go ask another quitter for help. Piece of cake, right?

Hopefully you will read on and learn some more about the "opportunities" that those of us in active addiction get to experience.

This is just the tip of the iceberg that needs to thaw.

3 GET MY BLISS ON

07.11.16

Blissfest... pfft...

Of all the horizon expanding, outside the box thinking, habit breaking bullshit I'm supposed to be doing, I am conned into going to Damn Dirty Hippie-fest. Let's go stand in the middle of a dusty, dirty field and sing protest songs and smoke dope in our bare feet. For those of you that know me, you know that is the description of my hell on Earth.

And you can bet your ass that they have dusty, dirty fields for hippies named "Okra" and "Gravel" and "Tallow" to frolic in and get filthy dirty while cursing the Man. Splendid. How did I find myself in this anti Brooks Brothers mess? Awesome friends, that's how. This will be a light read with a life lesson that my Dad taught me years ago but that I have only recently remembered due to my permanent time out with a certain style of beverage. Blissfest.

What the shit.

Never in a million years. Until fate tosses you in front of the Susan and Rocky train.

I met these two when I was slinging drinks for a local brewery and have thanked my lucky stars for them ever since. In the old days (a few years ago) I'd get to partake in a delicious beer or three and share great stories of conquest at sea (they are both sailors AND racers so they knew color was not only added but encouraged) and we would part ways.

The brewery was our only common meeting place and it stayed that way for quite awhile. Then something terrific happened. We started a Friday tradition of dinner after work.

Gourmet food from Happy's Tacos? (Seriously the best tacos on the planet)

Yes, please! And yes, the tacos are just as delicious with a black cherry cream soda as a beer. Rigorous testing has proven it.

One night, over a particularly delicious iced tea, Susan suggested that I join them at Dirtfield Dust Fest. I hesitated at first but the second lemon wedge kicked in and I caved.
Looks like iced tea is my new excuse for bad decisions. Two weeks fly by and it's time to pay the piper. I had to work for a few hours before Granola Kale Hemp Fest but I was ready.

Brought a change of clothes that I thought would help me blend in and of course, an older pair of sneakers that I was prepared to part with after they were destroyed in that infernal field!

Here is the ugly part of the story: I was trying to convince myself to bail. Instead of embracing the opportunity to try something new with some great people, my anxiety was building and trying to get me to retreat.

Find an excuse; there's going to be crowds, the people are going to be freaks, it's so damn hot you should just go sailing, it's a long drive, etc.

You know the real problem? It was different.
I don't do "different."

That was the only problem and that is an active symptom of my condition. I've embraced a lot of changes in these past few months of recovery but this was a giant leap. Remember jumping off the dock to your mom or dad, trusting them but not really?
That split second in the air when you wish you could somehow get back to that dock before you met your end in a watery grave?

Yep.
THAT is the feeling I had.

Guess what? Mom and Dad never dropped us.
One of the lessons that continues to be reinforced is that our true friends won't "drop us" either.

I had to force myself to jump off this dock and am so thankful that I did. *(I may have been pushed, the investigation is ongoing.)*

Here is a little known and definitely under-advertised fact about this festival. You are going to see people you know there. Lots of them. They are going to be just as glad to see you as you are them.

You are going to leave with more friends than you started with. Lots of them.

I got to see my good friend Jenny B before I even got through the will call process.

Rocky was showing me the grounds and I got to buy the coldest, most delicious water from my friend Kelsey at the Happy's Tacos truck.

A few more steps and a big hug from my friend Bob while Kathy was getting her tarot cards read.

Bob and Kathy are incredibly well respected members of our community. She was my son's teacher for crying out loud! This is how the festival works.

It's a music festival but SO much more. Imagine walking across your back yard, listening to amazing live music, the smell of some of the best food you can ask for wafting through the air and seeing some of your favorite people every few feet.

It's that incredible. Had it not been for Susan and Rocky, there is a 100% chance that I would have never experienced Blissfest.

I've discovered that people watching is a magnificent a sport to practice in recovery.

It was nice to be able to "drink" in the experience and let people just be people. In my drinking days, I would have been judging everyone that was different than me.
It would have made my inferior self feel superior.

Now I can enjoy the parts I like and let the other stuff go.

Did I see some goofy stuff? Goofy to me, sure.

Goofy to the people enjoying it?
Not at all. Did it bother me? Nah, I had my Bliss on.

4 CHOW VS DEREK

07.19.16

For those of you that don't know me, I've been a Superman fan since I was a very young man. This battle I'm about to describe is one of the more confounding ones for ol' Supes.

He's up against Bizzaro, the complete reverse persona of the Man of Steel, yet not totally evil. Before we get TOO far into this story, let me clarify something.

I am not saying I am either character, just using them to demonstrate. And because I think Superman is awesome. Oh, Batman is a brooding wannabe that has no super powers so don't go there.

Maybe the title should have been "Chow OR Derek". Maybe the two aren't mutually exclusive at all? Maybe I should just write a bunch of words and figure it out later?
Maybe some of my former English teachers are rolling their eyes and groaning because they will have to burn another red pen on one of my creative masterpieces!

This might help... One of the *"Old Timers"* said this in a Saturday morning meeting a while back, "Alcoholics are egomaniacs with inferiority complexes."

Opposites...opposing forces…equal and opposite… Aha!

Wait.

What the hell is that supposed to mean? It means we are in a constant state of internal conflict.

We don't really care for ourselves very much when you get right down to it.

It's not a case of constant self-loathing where that is all we think about.

No, it's more subconscious, and as your doctor through this journey, I will say it is far worse.

Water boarding for the soul. Internally we are in perpetual turmoil and not incredibly pleased with the fact that we can't fix ourselves.

People in active addiction are quite often very bright and are obsessive problem solvers.

We are born with bad wiring in the brain, emotionally a bit challenged AND smart enough to realize it. It is exhausting. Ready for a drink?
While you are pouring yourself one, I'm going to hammer down some of this Cherry Faygo Sparkling Water.

Almost as good as scotch from what I recall.

Chow VS Derek?
Chow OR Derek?

One more idea, Chow IS Derek and vice versa.
Or at least I am now.

Now they are both just names.

One my given name, one my nickname.

Before they were personas. And they were definitely different! Chow was a great cover for the insecure, inferior person that was originally named Derek.

Follow me for a second.

Chow lived in Chowenvoix, practiced religion in the Church of Chowentology, drank Chowzer beer (which I assume is still delicious), fixed things with a Phillips head Chowdriver, etc. I was the Chowzen one living in Chowtopia! And not ONE of those uses of my nickname from school was made up by me.

I'm surrounded by some clever people, huh? There are a bunch more that I'm not sharing but you get the idea. All that goofy, fun bullshit was awesome.

I totally fed off of it. It made me feel like part of the popular group. Ego? HUGE! Bulletproof! Years of people doing that type of stuff was a great band-aid for that cut up soul. Combine that with booze and that wound would heal eventually, right?

Derek... Who the hell is that?

It's still funny to hear people call me that to this day. When I first started AA, I swore I would be rid of the nickname "Chow."

Obviously that damn nickname was causing all the problems in my life. Derek was a safe way to go. Derek wasn't the raging party guy, it was that damn Chow! Yeah, let's get him! Pitchforks and torches time!

Right... just like soda is better than pop.

Turns out that Chow and Derek are the same guy now. And that is an accomplishment.

What's the point? I honestly forgot. I usually write out a schematic (I have been DYING to use that word) on a yellow pad, but not tonight.

If I was hanging out with you I could make up a point and just bullshit my way through it but writing won't let me do that.

How about this...

Quitting drinking is the ripping off of that dirty, disgusting band aid that allowed my soul/psyche to get infected and become someone that wasn't Chow OR Derek. Someone capable of doing shitty things with no regard for others or the consequences.

Almost five months of recovery has given me the gift of "sight." Seeing what I had become but the ability to cry plenty of healing tears to see what I could be again.

It is humbling and glorious.

5 "GO TO HELL..."

07.26.16

Imagine hearing your phone "ding" that you have a message. Imagine seeing that tiny blinking light. Nine times out of ten we are all excited to see what the message is, right?

Someone commenting on a silly picture you posted or wondering if you wanted to meet for a drink. Fun stuff, like normal people get all the time.

Now imagine this... Imagine that you made a giant mistake.

Try to think back to when you had to confess to something awful. You were caught. No way out. Stone cold busted.

Can you remember a time when you let someone down so completely that you thought the world was going to end? Take that moment, that horrible deed and start thinking about the feeling of being caught.

Now think about the feeling of, "How am I going to fix it?" Where to start? Who to start with? What to say? Got that sick feeling memorized?

Now imagine that you lied to everyone and told them you had brain cancer. The lie that I told.

That is exactly what I did.

This is the most awful chapter to write much less read. Yep, brain cancer. What the hell was that all about and where the hell did I come up with such an awful story?

Must have been the booze. I can blame everything on the booze, right? No. I can't. This one is all my fault and my responsibility. It has taken five months of recovery and countless hours of "chatting" with a brilliant guy from AA to be able to do this.

I'm sorry for the lie and sorry for the delay on this apology. There isn't a single one of you that deserved what I did. It wasn't designed to hurt anyone or get attention or sympathy. None of that.

Nope, it was so I could drink enough to kill the pain, self loathing, insecurities, etc. Normal people don't act like that. Normal people don't tell lies like that.
I was in a meeting with a friend a week or so ago and I had to disclose my actions to him. His comment slapped me in the face and actually helped me be able to write this.

"You told the lie but it wasn't Derek. It was your disease trying to survive."

This guy deals with such unfortunates on a daily basis so I trust his observation.

Here is a quick peek inside of where I was a few years ago.

Lots of you probably saw me at the brewery or on some sort of social media at the brewery because I was there a LOT. It was a good thing at the time.

I was fortunate to work for some great people in a fascinating business. What could be more exciting than being able to help start a brewery, in my favorite town right next to one of my favorite lakes?

I got to work with some great people and made some fantastic friends by just bringing them a beer. 70+ hours a week wasn't bad because you were shoulder to shoulder with your friends making things happen.

I got to watch my daughter learn the ropes and excel beyond all expectations at her first job. Idyllic! Except I was homeless.

I would go "home" to a loft in a friend's pole barn or sleep on a friend's boat.
Work your ass off for 16 hours then hide your truck so no one knew where you were living.
Sleep for a few hours then go back at it. I'm grateful for the people that helped me, no question about it.

A few months of inconvenience allowed me to finally get a place of my own. Now let the hours pile up and summer wear on.
Face the little girl that used to think you hung the moon and know that if she found out, she would be devastated.

Your son could come in for a beer and dinner but you couldn't invite him over for a cookout because there was no place to invite him to.

Oh, did I mention that my best friend on the planet was battling kidney cancer as well? Most of you know my best friend is my Dad.

Anyone out there see an issue with an alcoholic working at a brewery? Rivers of some of the most delicious beer I've ever tasted.

That industry is incredibly charitable as well. Any brewer that was rolling through town always stopped for a few and in turn, brought a few of their own creations. An infinite supply of "medicine" to numb the brain AND companionship to subdue the loneliness?

The most imperfectly perfect spot to be. The hours, the booze and the pain were taking their turn beating the shit out of me. In the end they conspired to defeat me.
I didn't start my day with a coffee or diet Coke anymore, it was beer.

It started to affect my performance. What to do? Ask for help? Hell no! Tell a story so big and so awful, no one would question you.

Fucking brain tumor.

That's what I came up with. Run with it through summer then the miracle of medicine would "cure" me and we could all move on like nothing happened or worst case scenario, let the “tumor” take me in the form of a .45 caliber bullet.

Lies that big always get busted. There are TONS of gory details but I will spare you those for now. That isn't the reason for this chapter.

The reason for the chapter is to admit, apologize and take full responsibility. I had to call my Mom and Dad and tell them what I had done.

I will never forget the feelings I had storming through me as I told my Dad, who actually had cancer, about my lie. Forty four years old and crying like a baby because you had just let down the two people that have endured endless sacrifice to raise you.

Having to face friend after friend, people that have become family over the years, and admit what I had done. All of this while trying to find recovery.
The support that I've been receiving during my journey to recovery has been tremendous and helpful but before I can truly accept it, you all deserve the truth. I own this. I'm reminded daily of my lie.

Facing friends that have cancer or know someone that does. I will never escape what I did.

Earned pain.

The title of this chapter? The ending words of a message from one of my formerly very favorite people after I admitted what I did and tried to apologize.

The ding of the phone might as well have been a gunshot and that little light a laser beam straight through my heart. I know I'll see more of those words and I am braced for it.

This is a necessary step in the rebuilding of Derek according to a very smart man. He hasn't failed me yet, so here we go.

6 THE RESERVOIR OF GOODWILL

08.02.16

The title. So deep. So thought provoking. Profundity must ensue! Nah, not in this episode. This is going to be an easy read because you all definitely deserve it and my creative get up and go just got up and went.

This chapter will be a quick examination of the intangible substance called "goodwill."

I always used to wonder why my Dad would wave to everybody that went by. Whether we were driving in the car or working on something in the yard, Dad always waved.

What little kid wouldn't want to know why Superman waved to everyone?

"Did you know him, Dad?" "Nope."

Hmm... "How about that guy? Did you know him?" "Nope."

Hmm... "How about THAT guy? Did you know him???" "Nope."

Oh come on!!! No more guessing.

No more trying to figure this out on my own, I'm just going to ask, dammit! (I'm a little kid and wasn't swearing at this point but I felt a little emphasis was needed right there.)

“Why do you wave to every single damn person that goes by???” *(I just threw that bad word in there because you can just imagine a frustrated 5 year old trying to figure this out)*

"Because it's nice to wave." The giant mystery of my Dad waving boiled down to, "Because it's nice to wave."

Guess what else I figured out by observing this phenomenon? Nice people wave back. Did my Dad wave because he expected the other person to wave back? Nope.

He did it because it was nice.

This observation pattern is generational as my kids used to be confounded in exactly the same way. My first lesson in goodwill was watching Dad wave for no other reason than "it's nice to wave."

I was fortunate to grow up with two of the most giving parents a kid could have. You were nice, kind, helpful, generous, etc not because you might get something from that person but because it was the right thing to do.

Ever stop to check on someone pulled over on the side of the road? Did you do it because you were expecting some cash?

Didn't think so. *Goodwill.*

Ever buy someone's lunch when you were ahead of them at the

drive through? Goodwill. Ever drag your ass out of bed at three in the morning to pull your friend out of the ditch? Goodwill.

(And usually a great story with an opportunity to rag on your buddy so that is a little selfish.) That's probably enough defining goodwill and if not, I will provide a link to an online dictionary.

I am going to use white as my font color so it will be a bit hard to see...

Now about that catchy title, "Reservoir of Goodwill". Thought long and hard about that one. Or I borrowed it from my AA meeting last Saturday morning.
It's really not important but the concept is. The guy that used the phrase was addressing a new guy that dragged himself in, just like I had so many months ago. Different circumstances but same result.

Not a single one of us walk through that door the first time on a winning streak.

New Guy told us his story.

Some of us nodded, some sipped their coffee but not one person judged. New Guy held back tears while he forced out his story. The Old Timers sat there and smiled and waited.

Once New Guy finished, lots of love and understanding was dispensed. Not one of us knew him but we heaped our support on him unconditionally. Nothing expected in return.

Guess what it was???? **Goodwill!!!**

New Guy screwed up and was forced in to the meeting but everyone was glad to see this stranger and help. No judging, no expectations, just help.

Because it was nice.

One of the *Old Timers* listened and let everyone chat then just quietly said,

> *"Welcome. Glad to see you here. You are safe here. Hopefully you come back. The things you did to get you here don't matter anymore. They will get repaired in time or they won't, you don't get to decide so don't worry about it. You just made a withdrawal from your reservoir of goodwill. The nice part is you are filling it up more than you are draining it by being here. We need you as much as you need us."*

Talk about waving to someone you don't know...

The chapter before this dealt with the biggest lie I ever told. Putting it out there for the world to see led to some very sleepless nights.

Turns out it was one of the most important actions I could have taken. I put a massive hole in my reservoir but I also witnessed something. My reservoir getting filled back up by people that wanted help or that were drawing strength because they weren't alone.

One gigantic blunder, one incredibly difficult chapter written and the reservoir not only wasn't drained but it was getting refilled. Can it withstand another hit like it just took? Thankfully, I'm on a path now that we won't have to find out.

The nice part is that it was there and that there is enough to share. Not because I want something in return.
Because it is the nice thing to do.

7 AIR BRAKES

08.09.16

What is on the literary menu tonight?In depth analysis with a side of reflection? Hilarious storytelling with a healthy life lesson for dessert?

Neither!

Tonight we are having my Mom's homemade chocolate chip cookies, hypothetically of course. Recovery has a funny way of reminding you what a bugger life can be without it and how cool it is with it.

It took me awhile to figure out what the *Old Timers* were talking about when they tried to explain to me that recovery isn't just not drinking.

Ya, sure. Ok. Maybe you quit a bit too late, *Old Timer.* I KNOW what it is. I'm such an idiot... Recovery is like Mom's chocolate chip cookies.

Perfect in every way.

The end.

That's the short version.

The long version includes Bugs Bunny cartoons and advice from my Dad. And Mom's cookie recipe. One of the funny things about recovery is how memories return. Sometimes unprovoked, sometimes triggered. Rarely at a convenient time.

They aren't always bad memories, often times they are good. They all make me shake my head.

This is a good one so please feel free to read on and think about cookies if you get bored. Saturday mornings! Cartoons!

Good ones! Mom told me that before I was old enough to go to school, I would get up early with Dad and watch cartoons with him before he went to work, then head back to bed.

A routine I wouldn't mind today! Loved cartoons. Didn't want to get up for school but Saturday morning was party time!

No cable out in the country so it was network cartoons for my sister and me. Sneak down the world's creakiest wooden stairs so as not to wake up the parents. Not because I didn't want to wake them but because I wanted to sneak some of those homemade cookies out of that cookie jar!

This was no ordinary cookie jar. This is one that Mom made in ceramics class. It was awesome, except on Saturday mornings... This cookie jar was tall and majestic and Mom made it so it was a symbol of pure goodness. The material it was made from was NOT pure goodness.

Quite the opposite. James Bond only wished he could lift that lid without making a sound.

Tall jar + tall counter + short little kid = a challenge!

If you didn't lift that lid up perfectly straight it would sound like you just rang the Liberty Bell hard enough to put another crack in it. I swear I'd have a mouthful of cookie and Mom would magically have transported downstairs to tap me on the shoulder.

“Did we somehow decide it was ok to have cookies for breakfast?”

“Nomph...” I don’t know how to spell the mouthful of cookies version of “no."

It's funny NOW... Cookie crumbs inclusive, I head to the living room for the best part of Saturday mornings. Superfriends and Bugs Bunny, baby!

Superfriends taught us that even though things could get bleak and the bad guys could get the upper hand, the good guys always win in the end.

Bugs Bunny taught us that coyotes should never be engineers, roosters talked funny and had a great deal of animosity toward dogs and that you could plug a hunter's gun with your finger and not have to worry about personal injury.

There's the memory: awesome childhood, cartoons that entertained (and secretly taught because if it would have been obvious, we would have watched the less entertaining Flintstones) and cookies.

Can you picture your Saturday mornings?

Now the adult part. You knew it was coming and don't pretend you didn't. *Father's day 2016.* Haven't had a drink in about 4 months but looking back, I'm not sure I was "sober."

Drove to Onaway to spend the day with my Dad. I was still feeling pretty shitty and embarrassed about myself. Forty four years old and just committed my largest screw up. Oh, and admitted that I was an alcoholic. I'm certain that it was a huge shock to my Dad, right? We dinked around and of course, Dad still loved me. Hell, it seemed like he even still liked me!
Things were going so well, let's push it and ask for advice! My lie has led to a situation.

An incredibly painful situation. For numerous parties.

Dad always seemed to have had the answers to all of my previous situations, why not this one? I asked my question.

"I don't know, son."

The exact four words I didn't want to hear. And rarely have from this man.

Alcoholism reduces grownups to children. When we finally give in and quit fighting, it's beautiful but terrifying.

We used to have all the answers and if we didn't, we had the comforting embrace of booze to make everything alright.
Goodbye comfort.

All I wanted Dad to do was **TELL** me what to do, not **TEACH** me what to do. It wasn't happening this time. I've been lucky to experience lots of things with my Dad.

One is flying with him. *I still think my Dad is a secret agent but I don't want to blow his cover.* Watching Dad fly is awesome.

Constantly monitoring the instruments, taking in the view and calmly chatting.

Key word: calmly.

"I guess I would say this, son. Treat this situation like you are landing a plane full of people. The problem is, this time one engine is dead and the other one is on fire. You can see the runway and it's possible to bring it home but you get one shot. Now is the time for calm nerves and a quiet mind. Panic or rash decisions will get you killed."

Huh. That sounds pretty easy.

Why didn't I think of that?

I didn't think of that because calm and quiet haven't always been two words that come to mind right away when describing my problem solving skills. What the hell does this have to do with Bugs Bunny?

You can't see the crystal clear ties I've made? This is probably going to make a lot more sense to me but there was an episode where that wascally wabbit was in a crazy situation with an airplane.

He was in a dive that was irrecoverable. Wings were bent back, airspeed indicator showing 5000 mph, etc. Our intrepid rabbit is pulling back as hard as he can on the stick and not a damn thing is helping.

The plane is about to smack the Earth when miraculously, it screeches to a halt.

Damned if that rabbit didn't step out and say, *"Heh, heh, heh. Air brakes."* I feel like I used the air brakes move. The problem in real life is that even though I didn't crash the plane, I didn't make it an easy flight for my passengers (friends and family) and the landing has done some serious damage to THEM.

There are a few that won't "fly" with me again and I have to accept that.

There are some that I banged up pretty badly but with time, effort, humility and sincerity, I hope to soar together again.

Time for a cookie.

Maybe two.

8 PUTTING A REEF IN MY LIFE

08.17.16

"Control is an illusion, you infantile egomaniac. Nobody knows what's going to happen next: not on a freeway, not in an airplane, not inside or own bodies and certainly not on a racetrack with 40 other infantile egomaniacs." - Nicole Kidman in Days of Thunder

What does a quote from one of the most accurate racing documentaries of all time have to do with lines on a sailboat?

I'm a little surprised that you had to ask but I'll try and help you out.

In all honesty, Days of Thunder was one of the LEAST accurate racing movies ever made but that quote has stuck with me for 25+ years.

You can substitute anything you want for "infantile egomaniac" and your situation doesn't need to be a racetrack but I'm guessing we can all identify with the ass-chewer and the ass-chewee.

No, I don't know the proper spelling of the two words involving said berating but my audience is sophisticated enough to figure it out.

See, the ass-chewer is the person administering the ass chewing and...never mind.

Alcoholics are definitely egomaniacs. Infantile at times for certain. More often than not, we are some of the most insecure egomaniacs you'll ever run across.

Some of you can see through the bravado and bullshit, some can't. It is damn near impossible for us to admit that we are insecure and are not in control.

Our arrogance forces us to spend so much time lying to ourselves that we ARE actually in control and secure that we start to believe it.

That belief, as faulty and wrong as it may be, is our invisible shield. Knowing full well that you are all rabid Star -Wars fans just like I am, you understand that shields take energy.
Non-addicts get to refill your emotional energy with such foolish things as going for walks, reading books, spending time with loved ones, etc.

We alcoholics just have to pour a drink and that action alone starts the regeneration process. Right. Now for the sailboat reference and what is this "reef" I speak of... not just yet.

Prep work first... Try to visualize learning something that you badly wanted to do. Ride a bike, learn to swim, roller skate, etc.

Every one of those things requires control. Riding a bike? Balance, hand eye coordination and the ability to trick your brain into turning the handlebars right to go left (try turning right to go right sometime.)

My Mom and Dad must have run a million miles teaching me to ride my bike as I had no balance or coordination. Riding into the massive maple tree in the front yard comes to mind.

Got that bike going and I was damned sure not going to stop! The tree had other opinions... Eventually I got the hang of it and got some "control."

That element of control was freedom.

Remember learning to swim? I will always remember the day my daughter was walking around the edge of the pool and said, "I just want to swim so bad, daddy."
A few million cannonballs and countless gallons of spit in my face later, that perfect little goggle faced girl learned to swim. And gained some control. And that precious freedom.

Roller skating? Pretty obscure and it obviously dates me but yep, roller skating.

My parents separated and I moved to a new school in 5th grade.

One of the things the "city kids" did was go to the roller rink and skate in a giant circle.

My mastery of the bicycle did NOT transfer to skating. My skating “technique” was more walking around the rink with wheels on my feet.

Oh, and if I accidentally did get rolling, there was a stupid wheel looking thing turned sideways on the front of the skate to put an immediate halt to that!

Two determined girls named Karrie and Betsy dragged me

around that rink (patiently, mind you) until I could skate. At least when the circle was going counter clockwise. Control. Freedom. See the trend here? Sailing...

A fantastic activity that you can do solo or with friends. Racing or cruising. Lots of options and an almost infinite number of variables to control. The sails are constantly in need of trim if you want to get maximum performance out of the breeze you are given.
Or you could just set them close and enjoy the experience. You are in control.

Every boat is different but the principles are the same. There are all kinds of lines (ropes for you non-sailors) on a sailboat. They all have their own jobs. Some are to take sails up and down, some are to let sails in and out.

Halyards, sheets and tack lines, oh my!

Then there are specialty lines. Lines used a little less often. Lines like reefing lines.

Reefing lines are used to reduce the sail area of the mainsail when the wind starts to pipe up. Less sail area gives you more control of your boat, let's her stand up a bit straighter and makes for a more comfortable journey for everyone on board.

After being on this planet for forty plus years, I finally realized that control IS an illusion.

To a point. I can only control MY actions and reactions to outside forces.

That's it. Can you imagine the weight off my shoulders knowing that and more importantly, accepting it? Freedom.

The compulsion to control everything BUT myself is gone.
Oh that asshole that pulls out in front of me and drives 2mph still pisses me off once in awhile but not as often as it used to.

(Secretly I still mutter "asshole" under my breath but more often than not, it's with a smile on my face. Please don't be that asshole.)

Can't control him, so don't worry about it. Putting down the bottle has allowed me to put a reef in my life.

There's a bit more control (of myself), I can stand up a bit straighter and based on extensive surveys, the journey for everyone on my "boat" is more comfortable.

I still need my friends and family more than ever and fully realize I didn't get to this good place without you dragging me around the roller rink we call life.

9 I MADE IT! WHERE AM I?

08.22.16

According to my incredibly accurate record keeping aka an app on my phone, it has been six months since I have taken a drink of alcohol. Yahoo!!! I finally made it!!! Yep, I made it...to...the most disappointing day of this entire journey.

And now that I am far enough away from the self-pity party caused by that mean old day I can pull it apart and see why it was such a bummer.

Six months ago I looked at my "roommate" and told him I was done drinking. He shared some insight with me. The ups and downs of getting sober. Was AA a useful program? If sobriety was so good why did he give it up?
This is also the time "the lie" was discovered so life as I knew it was about to change forever. I'd quit drinking before, for three months, why not just do it again? First things first, might as well get rid of this fifth of rum first. No need for that kind of temptation once I quit, right?

Turns out, drinking that last fifth of rum was the right thing to do. I felt like garbage but not a full can, maybe just one of the little ones you have in your bathroom.

To the untrained drinker, that is a bad sign. That should have been a crippling hangover.

A few beers, a fifth of rum and I'm guessing no dinner because food wasn't a priority toward the end. Drag my ass out of bed, shower the booze off of myself and head to AA. Only I can't quite find the balls to go in. *(See Chapter 2 "100 Laps")*

Can't admit to that failure so I head to the frozen boat launch for an hour.

The cold air was a good assist for putting out the flames of embarrassment.

Fast forward a bit...a couple months, tops. Now I'm not the *"new guy"* in the meetings.

One morning the next new guy snuck in and joined us. Oddly enough, he too struggled with walking in that door. Maybe the doorknob is messed up... We welcomed him and listened to his story. I was still so excited about how awesome I was for quitting that I couldn't wait to talk! Then one of the *Old Timers* spoke. "The only thing we ask of you here is that you only come in if you want to quit drinking. If you don't want to quit or aren't sure, go out and drink some more. You'll know when you are ready."

Wait a minute! I didn't get to expound on how much I learned and profoundly change this man's life!

Damn you, *Old Timer*!

Guess who learned a few things that day?
1) My enthusiasm, while appreciated, was more *tolerated* than

anything. I was no different than any other newbie.

2) I had consumed enough. The Old Timer's words were perfectly assembled and perfectly timed.

3) Two months was a huge accomplishment but I needed to recalibrate my timeline of success benchmarks. The days fly by. The weeks fly by. Now the months are even starting to pick up steam.

Reading my journal from the beginning to now makes me wince.

The stupid stuff that I wrote down as "important" serves as a flashing neon sign reminder of how bad things were.

The only constant from Day 1 to today is the alcoholism.

Lots of reading, research and meetings have helped me start to understand this thing. Booze is just a part of it. Wanna know why my Sunday was SO disappointing? Wanna know why I had the blues? Listen and learn (and feel sorry for me) people.

Had coffee with a good friend from a lifetime ago. Had a surprise lunch with my dear friends, Mike and Nancy. Someday they will each get a chapter all their own, that's how huge they are to me.

Talked to my Mom for almost an hour. She is kicking some serious butt post shoulder surgery, *thank you for asking.* I'll let her know you all said, "Hi Mom!"

Called my Dad after I recharged my phone battery. (Sorry Mom, I love you!)

Guess what? Dad is killing it, too! I get to have lunch with him Wednesday. Dad said to tell all of you "hello" and thanks for taking care of his kid.

Got to see the Professor and his gal for some laughs AND picked up my bike! Yes I cleaned it up last night, Johnny.

SEE!?!? A shitful day!

Because I didn't stay outside of myself.

I built the six month anniversary into some magic day filled with balloons and cakes and dragons and race cars and jet flyovers. That's the selfishness of the disease creeping to the front again.

Instead of being overwhelmed by how fortunate I am to have so many great friends and be able to talk to BOTH of my parents, I was pissy because the parade didn't happen.

Picture me standing at the end of my driveway, stupid party hat on, stupid pinwheel in one stupid hand and a stupid sparkler that won't light because the stupid lighter won't light it in my other stupid hand and a pile of stupid confetti on the stupid ground. Pretty stupid, huh?

Here comes the good part.

The gift that is recovery let me figure out what was wrong instead of firing some cubes into my favorite glass and filling it with "medicine."

I was being a selfish prick.

I had a fantastic day that some people would kill for. So tonight, I drink some sugar-free, certainly poisonous, raspberry Kool-Aid in my formerly favorite rocks glass with a single Death Star ice cube and say thank you to each of you.

I don't know how some people fight this disease alone because it truly takes the army that is YOU to keep me on track. I would not be here without you.

Gratitude and humility to the nth degree.
So where am I?

Six months into the journey of a lifetime.

Right where I am supposed to be.

P.S. I have plenty of stupid party hats if anybody needs one. :)

10 WHAT IS YOUR SPIRITUAL ALTITUDE?

08.28.16

How 'bout that title, eh? Made that one up all by myself! This chapter is going to lightly touch on spirituality. What it means to me, what I think it is and just some observations on how my spirituality continues to change.

I've been noticing a souring of my attitude lately and there isn't a good reason for it. Things are not perfect by any stretch but they are better than they have been in a long time.

You could probably say that things are actually pretty normal.

Condition Normal is foreign to me, and potentially dangerous. The horrible lows of "morning" are gone but so are the extreme highs of "night."

No hangovers, getting out of bed and watching the sunrise, remembering what you did and said the night before and your wallet not being mysteriously destroyed are all pretty good things, right?

Uproarious laughter, shenanigans and story making were pretty good things too, right? The answer to both questions is of course, "Sometimes."

I'm not sure if manic is the right word but I'm going to insert it here because it sounds very doctor-ish and adds validity to this chapter. If I described my brain as "thrashing," it would sound less doctor-ish, although incredibly accurate.

The thrashing brain. That could be a title on its own. Things are so great I can hardly stand it!!! Why is everything so shitty??? I'm so lucky!!! Why does this always happen to me???

Sound exhausting? Maybe just a tiny bit?

Alcohol used to balance out those swings. What I didn't want to admit was that the swing balancing was an illusion. A temporary masking. God, it felt good. Damn- the price I would eventually pay.

Short-term, please just give me some peace. Let me feel that calm that non-addicts feel. Help me make my smile feel real. Round those peaks of euphoria and sadness off a bit so neither one can cut me anymore. Can't cry if I keep myself dehydrated, now can I?

Disgusting.

Can you see why some addicts will never quit using their drug of choice?

It's terrifying to think about giving up your "medicine"."

The only thing that gives you peace.

"Ok, here's the deal, Mr. Chowen. You quit drinking and your life is going to improve immeasurably."

Why not just say, "Ok, here's the deal, Mr. Can't Swim. Quit paddling around with your life jacket on and your life is going to improve immeasurably. If you don't die first."

Sounds like a pretty good time to get spiritual, doesn't it? Well what the heck does that mean and where do you buy spirituality?

God-mart hasn't opened a store in Charlevoix or the surrounding towns. You are in luck, reader. After minutes and minutes of intense study and research, I know what spirituality is. First, it's free. Second, it's different for everyone.

Please mail your tuition payments to me immediately.

Here is where I expound on spirituality.

My theory is quite groundbreaking... *It's whatever you need to get by.* NOBODY but YOU can define it for you. Boom.

If God lifted your compulsion to drink, I couldn't be happier for you. If it was the alien spacecraft full of visitors, good on you.

Whatever. It. Takes.

For me, it's a lot of things. I like writing. Sometimes. I like going for a walk. Sometimes. I like sailing. Pretty much anytime. Spirituality is anything I can grab a hold of and quiet my mind.

I make my daily pilgrimage to the lake at least twice a day. Love the sunrise just as much as the sunset. Sometimes I sit there for 5 minutes, sometimes it's an hour.

Whatever it takes.

Something I've learned over the past six months is that there is no single "correct" way to do this recovery thing. Reading my journal from the first three months showed how I hard I thrashed, grabbing on to every idea as though it was the best one and I better use it or else I would surely fail.

The further I get from my last drink and the more I practice the quiet mind, the better things get. The more visits the lake received yesterday, the higher my spiritual altitude rose.

Enough introspection allowed the ballast tanks of daily life to be purged of sour attitude and replaced with fresh the fresh air of gratitude. I can still experience uproarious laughter, shenanigans and story making, I just don't feel compelled to.

I'm no longer defined by those things and I am happier for it. The beautiful mornings aren't the disappointment of an unfulfilled night, they are the gift of an evening well spent.

It's really peaceful at proper spiritual altitude. The fasten seatbelt sign has been turned off and you are free to move about your life.

11 A PLUNGE INTO DARKNESS

09.05.16

I'm kind of laughing as I write this at 5:00 Labor Day afternoon... This chapter actually started yesterday morning at about 8 bells.

Several shiny objects later, I'm back to actually sit my butt down and write it.

So here we go... BOOF! It's a very dramatic word signifying a very dramatic sound effect for a very dramatic event.

I'm sorry if you weren't prepared for such drama.

I'll let you collect yourself while I set the scene that led to such shock and awe... Saturday was filled with aggressive recreating.

A full day on the sailboat watching the Red Fox regatta unfold culminating in an impromptu pizza party with my friends and my favorite 5 year old.

I was hitting the cherry sparkling water pretty hard and even had a diet Dr. Pepper with my pizza.

Tough stuff, right?

I've been training for such days all my life so please don't be concerned. I've come to realize that this journey is partly mental and partly physical.

This learning moment was a combination. I've recently been introduced to a new physiological condition called "hydration."

Unlike whizzing when you are drinking because you are in the process of dehydrating, whizzing when you are drinking cherry sparkling water means you are full. Yep, hydrated!

Light bulb moment numéro uno. Light bulb moment number one led directly to light bulb moment number two. Light bulb moment number one was mental; light bulb moment number two was physical. Going to bed at an incredibly late 11pm and even "checking" (every parent reading this has told their child to "check" so you know what I mean) still resulted in an unfortunate 5:12am slumber interruption.
You know... I had to take a whiz!

The reason I remember the exact time? My alarm clock was the only light inside or outside of my place. And the last thing I could see for hours...

Back to the important task at hand. I take the memorized steps to the appropriate door, turn left, hit the switch and BOOF!

The supernova that was once a 60 watt bulb exploded with blinding brilliance then was no more.

Blinded by the light and having to whiz bad enough to get out of bed at 5:12am are two things I hope you never experience in unison. The sink and shower were options considered, trust me. Not used but considered.

Little known fact I'm happy to share... light bulbs rarely burn out in the daytime and NEVER explode when your bladder is empty.

It's science, people. *Just accept it.*

There is the back story.

Now on to the brilliance of my stupidity. How many times do you think I flicked that switch expecting that magical light bulb to fire up? You know for a fact I didn't change it right away. After all, it was getting light out after I woke from my 5:17am nap. It didn't occur to me that it might get dark again... Click. Dammit. Click. Rats. Click. Seriously? Click. I'm an idiot. Click. Change the bulb, dimwit! *(pun intended)*

Probably best I live alone lest I be committed for chatting with myself.

I know for sure at least one of you has done this. Pretty please just someone say they have. What's the point of the light bulb fiasco?

It's actually a big one. One of the things I've learned about my condition is that a lot of my drinking was habit or situationally based.

Obviously the underlying brain stuff was always there but a bunch of it was just plain habit.

Get home from work? Put on tunes and pour a drink. Go to a friend's house for dinner? Visit while I mix drinks. Finish a sailboat race? Grab the cooler, distribute beverages and crack a cold beer. Flick that switch! Nothing different would happen.

I'd drink just like always. Not always to a shit-facing but it's been determined that zero drinks is the proper amount so any was too much. Mind numbed, I didn't see the problem.

Now that I'm successfully in recovery? Hell yes it's time for a beer! Oooohhhh wait, no it isn't.
It's time for anything BUT a beer. And it would take a second or two to process. It's getting more and more rare but it happens.

Bad Derek! No beer! Change that bulb.

Now I'm far enough away from my last adult beverage that the new way is becoming more natural.

I don't have to be worried about being surprised then make a conscious decision to NOT grab the beer or whatever else is in front of me.

I'm not foolish enough to think that all of the burnt out bulbs have been changed or that some of the dimmer ones won't need to be replaced with brighter versions.

The nice part is that I'm figuring out what happens when I flick the switch on the shiny new bulbs and it's pretty exciting. *The darkness is going away.*

If you see me hesitate for a second when normally I wouldn't, I'm probably just changing a bulb.

I'll be done in a second or two.

12 THE FULCRUM OF SERENITY

09.10.16

Who would ever expect to receive brilliant advice on a bar napkin in an AA meeting?

I have done countless deals on these miniature contracts. How many times had I written an important event on one? Things so important that I didn't want to forget them but not quite important enough to leave my seat at the bar.

Funny sayings? I've got a million of them! Well, I did but they were written on those tiny little notepads and many went through the wash.

I do however, have one that will NEVER go through the wash. It is a treasure that is part of my memorabilia of success.

And failure, I suppose... I walked in to my meeting early so I could get a good seat.

Close to the door but not with my back to it. I could escape if things got "too hot" but not vulnerable where someone could sneak up on me.

Right. If things got "too hot" in an AA meeting.

The safest possible place I could be at that time.

Sat down, got my cup of coffee, my notepad and a pen. Everything squared to the table.

Neat and tidy. All set. Still in control.

Said hello to some familiar faces. Some that have become incredibly important people in this new life. (Hi, Sue! Congrats on 5 years!)

In the door walks this beautiful woman that looked SO familiar. Now I felt like I was sitting on an airplane during boarding.

100 supermodels and one guy that just won the world hot dog eating contest.
Come on, come on andddddd..... Nice to meet you, Champ. Have a seat. But not this time! She sat next to me! And said, "Hi!"

Using my name! Oh no! Where did I know her from???
The meeting unfolded and I listened carefully so when it was my turn to talk, I would have the most profound story and leave everyone speechless at how far I'd come since last week. There's that self-centered egomaniac!

I shared my brilliant insights and observations and received the expected praise.

Later I find out that the praise is given to every newbie. Because we are all self-centered egomaniacs to a point and until we figure that out, the *Old Timers* tolerate us as best they can because they truly want us to come back.

The pretty lady to my right asked to use my pen and grabbed what I find out is just a napkin. Not a bar nap or a cocktail nap, just a little square napkin. Same dimensions as the familiar bar naps, same material, same everything except totally different.

These people on the inside put their coffee cups on the damn things for Christ's sake! I gave her my pen and watched her start to draw something.

Oh well, not for me. She heard something she didn't want to forget. She heard something alright, and didn't want to forget to share.

Ten-ish years prior to this meeting, we actually met at the shared pool of a group of condos on Round Lake in town. My family used to share a condo with a friend for the month of July. It was a great spot for us to spend time with friends and family and feel like we were on vacation in our own town.

One afternoon we were soaking in the sun and splashing around in the pool. This nice lady and her family joined us in the fun. She had a little guy that was turning 2. Cute as a bug. This little fella was fascinated by the pool. Fascinated but wary. His mom would bring him to the edge then take him back to the table.

Grandpa and Grandma were at the table and offering snacks and other distractions but this little bugger was pool focused.

I knew the grandparents well and waved hello. I waded over to the edge of the pool to see if he wanted to splash a bit while grandma held on to him. We did that for a bit while grandma and I chatted.

I love kids so I held my hands out to see if he wanted to come in and paddle around. He came to me and we waded around, feeling the water and "chatting."

The little shaver didn't have any words as I figured out but he sure could communicate. I noticed grandma back at the table with this guy's mom and dad and there were tears. It turns out my new little pal was autistic. To me, this was playing with my friend's grandson, to them it was a breakthrough.

This is where the expectations thing comes in. Sorry for the long windedness of this chapter but it's Friday night, I'm happily writing and the back-story is critical.

The pretty lady sitting next to me was the mom from the pool. Her son made a huge step that day. His fascination with water exists to this day. Her expectations for him were the same as any mom. Wanting the best for your kid is natural. She had her expectations in check.

She wanted a happy, healthy boy and anything like the day at the pool was over and above.

An awesome way to look at things. Did her expectations jump from time to time? Just like any parent? Absolutely.

The note she wrote on her napkin? It looked like a teeter totter. On one end it had the word “expectations” written and the other end had the word “serenity."

She then drew little arrows to show how the device worked. As expectations rose, serenity dropped. As expectations dropped, serenity rose. She learned to manage her expectations because she had to. Acceptance brought her serenity.

The extra stuff, the unexpected breakthroughs are frosting. She drew that picture to help me ease my mental thrashing. She saw the disguised agony and complete lack of peace.

When we first "come in" we don't come in on a winning streak. There is no serenity at first. Thawing out is painful.

Seeing my expectations and serenity were directly connected was a breakthrough. A few chapters back, I talked about how doing things for people not because you expect things in return but because it is nice. A nice act performed 10 years ago became a nice act received today.

Did I expect that? Heck no but what great frosting. This fulcrum of serenity is not exclusive to people in recovery. It applies to everyone. Lots of the stuff I'm learning does.

Breakthrough on a bar nap.

13 YOU ARE BEING WATCHED

09.21.16

Took a little break from writing to work on some new things called "feelings." The fortunate and unfortunate side effects of sobriety.

I used to have the perfect cure for the damn things but it turns out that the self prescribed medicine was deadly while these feeling things are actually ok to experience.

Who knew?
Dr. Chowen has been reported to the medical board for peer review.

Today we are going to discuss the paradox of wanting attention and being terrified of being watched.
Some of the previous chapters have touched on the topic of alcoholics being egomaniacs with inferiority complexes.

This chapter might help explain that piece of the condition and hopefully give you a few laughs as well. I walked into my first AA meeting with my head held high and greeted everyone at the table like I was running for office or...I snuck in like OJ Simpson after a quick stroll around the ole' neighborhood.

You know which one was true. The first few meetings were pure survival. Trying to break the cycle, the habits and hurry up and fix everything so I could get on with the show.

This is a process, things take time, keep coming back, blah, blah, blah. Where's my certificate of completion? I'm very busy...

Once I got past my ignorance/arrogance there were actually important things to be learned.

"You are being watched," one of the *Old Timers* said to me. He was trying to prepare me for a level of scrutiny that I hadn't experienced before.

Of course I was being watched, that's why I snuck in. But who the hell would watch me, I'm a nobody.

The paradox.

Years ago I used to race cars with/against my Dad. He is an excellent driver with a passion for racing combined with incredible talent and experience.

Should be easy to beat after I take a few practice laps, right??? My very first race, I qualified *dead last*. Slowest car out there.

The good part about that was I got to start right out front. Where hundreds of people could watch. An egomaniac's dream.

All the other drivers told me to just go out and have fun and they would go easy on me. Such fine fellows!

These guys are the best! Warm up laps are going well.

Racing is easy! Go really fast and hang out with your pals! Wow. Sure are a lot of people in those stands.

Cars are really bunching up for this start. Can't see much with this helmet on.

The sun is right in my eyes going in to turn one. Did I leave the iron plugged in?

Green flag! Mash that gas pedal, Chowen! It is a "race" car as the guys on the crew would remind me.

Usually as I washed and waxed the shiny car... Off we go! I'm a racecar driver! Woo hoo!

In to turn one and I'm in the front. Because that's where the slow cars start. Start my turn and nail the brakes and...accelerate?

What the heck??? There was no turning or slowing down. I just got the "rookie push."

Right off the track. I collected myself, got my car re-fired and drove around to my pit stall while my new "best pals" raced.

Sons a... I had all the attention an egomaniac could ask for just for racing but now people were watching.

Didn't realize the difference back then. I was pissed and embarrassed! Until the guys all came in and laughed at me. Then I knew it was going to be OK. The verbal tirade I had planned didn't happen, thank God.

Some of those guys are best pals to this day and that story gets better every year. Time for the next race.

Think people are watching? Think I care whether or not I left the iron plugged in?

I was NOT getting shoved off the track this time.

No sir!

I got black flagged before the start and sent to the back because I was trying to start the field TOO FAST! At least I got to race the damn thing and I didn't get lapped. Pretty eventful first day of racing, huh?

Large dose of humility administered that day.

Funny as hell to look back and see how pissed I was over stuff that meant nothing. That look back helps me figure out the difference between wanting to be the center of attention and being watched.

Why did the Old Timer tell me that I was being watched? Because I am. We all are to a point. Addiction is a mysterious condition. I'm immersed in this thing and I learn more about it every day. Some people are watching because they love you. They are rooting for you, whether publicly or privately. Good people want people to succeed. Some people are watching because they are curious.

This disease/condition is insidious and it touches more people than we think. They are trying to figure out what we do in our "secret" meetings and if it really works.

Some are watching because they are the ones that slow down to stare at a car crash. They want to see the ugly part. The ugly they see in others temporarily masks the ugly they see in themselves.

Others are watching because they are like me. Yep.

Just like me.

That last group of observers is why I chose to make my journey public. I like to write. It's fun when I'm doing it for the right reasons. *(A HUGE thank you to my friend Rhonda for that reminder!)* I don't want anyone else to go through what I've been through and more importantly, what I've put others through. If a little public humiliation helps some people, then it's totally worth it. The *Old Timers* tell me it's none of my damned business what other people think about me anyway. Try convincing yourself of that one. I'm amazed at how many people have reached out and continue to do so. It's a humbling experience.

Much like a rookie's first night on a race track, I suppose. Something happened recently to prompt this chapter and it justifies any and all embarrassment. A dear friend of mine that has been with me every ugly (and beautiful) second of this journey shared this with me the other day.

Her husband has been watching this little project I've taken on called sobriety. We men don't talk about this stuff much. We don’t talk about it because we are men and men don't talk about feelings.

Common knowledge, people... This guy has been reading my writings and talking stuff over with his wife throughout my adventure.

The other day, he hired a guy from my group. The details have to stay tight because of our small little town but suffice to say, that guy’s life just took a major step in the right direction.
Someone else stuck their neck WAY out to give that guy a second chance because he has a better understanding of what "addicts" are. Good on you, sir.

Thank you for taking a chance on that guy.

Our job as people in recovery and I would go so far as to say good people, is to pay it forward. We are there for the next person in the door. Doesn't matter to me if you walk in that door or just watch from the stands.

I'm happy to help. Let's get you to your green flag.

14 IGNORE ME DOING THIS

09.26.16

One of the things I hear a lot is, "I never knew." Well of course you didn't. Because I didn't want you to. I only let you see what I wanted you to see because I was in control.

Remember that chapter about the infantile egomaniac? At the end I was so far out of control I'm pretty sure you could tell.

Disguising behavior or hiding weakness is instinct. At least that's what the smart people tell me. Most of us hate conflict and will do whatever we can to avoid it. It isn't fun, it takes a lot of energy and usually no matter who "wins", there is damage to all involved.
I have some case studies to back this theory. Personal experience. There we were. My little sister and I. I was about 5 so Heather would have been about 3.

Back in the old fashioned days, TVs used to have things called "knobs" on them. These "knobs" were used to change between the many channels (four to be exact). Heather and I were not supposed to touch the knobs while Dad was watching the boring news.

Mind you, Mom probably chased us around the house with a wooden spoon for twelve hours while Dad worked the same or more hours and they MAY have just wanted 30 minutes of quiet time together before it was Dad's turn to administer the beatings.

Not sure. Disclaimer: Heather and I were not beaten. That was a story "enhancer".

Back to the TV... "Don't touch that." That was Dad advising me on channel selection. Reaching out one more time confirmed that he indeed did NOT want the knob touched.

What I misunderstood or ignored was that he wasn't concerned as much with the knob being touched as he was the channel being changed.

So being quite a bit smarter than Dad, I simply backed up to the knob, reached behind my back and gave that bad boy a turn! I was shocked at the next series of events! Dad knew instantly!
Wizard! The appropriate punishment followed. Heather's technique was slightly different. Same setup. Different evening. "Don't touch that." Sneaking to avoid conflict wasn't exactly her plan. She stood there, looking at Dad, cranking that knob like she was winding a clock! Two different approaches, same result.

Conflict? Screw that! At least I didn't experience instant justice! Better to be sneaky and live to turn the knob another day.

The thing I didn't realize was even though I thought I was all clear, I was busted. Love that story. Much funnier when my Dad tells it.

Fast forward a couple years... I was a budding electrical engineer.

Age 6 or 7.

Those of you that know me, know that I now tend to call the power company to cut power to my place when I change a light bulb.

A breaker is thrown at bare minimum. Not in the olden days. Ever watch someone take two bare wires (no plug) and stick them into a wall socket? Voila!

Whatever used to have a plug, works like normal! Albeit a lot more dangerously. One Saturday morning, I was conducting experiments in my laboratory aka the parlor. The reason this room was used should be pretty obvious.

It was close to the TV for Saturday morning cartoon viewing yet as far away as possible from prying eyes of my parents. They did their best to keep me alive and reasonably scar free. "Pop!"

Well that isn't what happens when Dad plugs light bulbs directly into the wall with no plug. Hmm... The reason it never happened to him was because he never plugged a mercury switch into the wall.

The "light bulb" I decided to mess with was plug free for a reason! Quick science lesson... Mercury is a shiny silver, liquid METAL that apparently conducts electricity incredibly well.

This "light bulb" was a switch from a thermostat. It wasn't designed to be plugged directly into a wall outlet. That shiny metal created an instant short and it blew. In my defense, it was super cool liquid metal inside of glass that looked like a tiny light bulb.

And I wasn't an electrical engineer. Uh oh... Dad's coming. That pop must have been louder than I thought! "What was that?"

Anybody want to guess the most universal response used by every kid from the beginning of time???

"Umm...nothing?"

Every single one of you said that out loud or in your head. Admit it, it's ok. "Nothing" made a very loud pop. Totally believable. Just go about your business and I'll take care of these two silly wires that were never hooked to anything much less plugged into the wall. Apparently a mercury switch vaporizes the glass bulb as well as the mercury it formerly held. It also turns a nasty black color, or so I've heard.

Here's Dad, standing over his super genius son claiming “nothing” made that loud noise. The problem with my story was the evidence to the contrary.

Picture the cartoon of the mad scientist that just blew something up in his lab.

All you can see is two white, blinking eyeballs and a face full of black, vaporized mercury and glass.

Nothing to see here, sir! Pretty sure he was almost fooled... and me without a scratch. Sneakily turning that knob and blowing up a mercury "light bulb" and I thought I could get away with both!

I didn't get away with either one of course.

I know I write in generalities about alcoholics quite a bit and I hope it doesn't bother anyone.

Some traits are similar but none are exact other than the fact that we can't drink.

At all.

Hard to get my arms around that sometimes. Easier to just accept it and tell funny stories. Did my Dad know I changed the channel and blew up that switch? Instantly on both occasions. Did some people know I had a rather sizeable issue with alcohol? Absolutely. No question.

Probably more than I will ever know.

And that's OK.

I avoided admitting it to escape conflict. The problem with that line of thinking is that subconsciously, I knew it had to be dealt with.

And that it was going to hurt.

The part I hate most is the hurt I caused more than the hurt I felt. As my pre-mortem brain exam continues by Angry Jimmy Buffet (my guy that is figuring me out) I learned that "The Lie" was built to fail. I was tired of running and designed something so stupid that I couldn't help but get caught.

Has the conflict that I caused hurt both sides? No question.

Do I wish I would have quit years ago?

I work on my time machine every night after work.

Do I appreciate the anger as much as the kindness?

I don't like it as much but I appreciate it just the same.

My goal is to help people put down that "light bulb" before it gets plugged in. I could have been blinded by that stupid stunt.

Please don't make my Dad get after you.

He has his hands full with me.

15 AUTOPILOT – DISENGAGED

10.04.16

Something pretty cool happened Saturday morning at coffee. I learned something! I learned that that the learning doesn't ever stop if you don't want it to.
So what brilliant gem did I glean from this meeting that I had to share? It was a one-two punch of "learn stuff" and "apply the stuff you learned, Chowen" that turns out I really needed.

One of the many rituals of this secret society is to ask about anniversaries and to congratulate each other on the accomplishments, whether it be one day sober or 40 years of long term recovery.

Everybody that cared to, announced their days-months-years sober and got their much deserved congrats. The moderator of the meeting looked at another guy and asked him if he wanted to tell us about his milestone. 33 years.

That's all.

Seriously?

He didn't say anything about his 33 years because he didn't feel like he was working the program.

Huh. He didn't feel like he was working the program so he didn't feel he had earned the praise. I guess the nice part about AA is you are allowed to pick and choose the pieces that work for you.

I'm thinking 33 years looks pretty good when I just cracked 7 months but we are all different and it matters not what I think.

The learning part... "Jim" wasn't happy with how he was working the program. He believed he had become complacent.

Again, I say, "huh". I honestly think I go to AA more for advice on how to live a happier life than to quit drinking. Dumping the booze was the easiest part by far. Some say that for those of us with the gift of alcoholism, drinking is 5% of the condition and the other 95% is mental. I'm cool with that ratio.
I had become just like "Jim." Complacent. Flying on autopilot. And I was bored. Not because I have nothing to do but because I have removed the psychological peaks and valleys experienced from enjoying adult beverages.

Some call it peace or serenity or normalcy.

I call it dangerous and can't thank "Jim" enough for pointing out the slippage. The center of the universe condition had found its way back in and quite stealthily taken over operations of the ole brain.

This was the perfect day to learn stuff. There was plenty of windshield time ahead this day. Going to Onaway to have lunch with Dad then to Boyne Mountain to see my friends, Justin and Annette then back home.

Kind of scheduled meeting times with breaks in between to work on this whole complacency thing. I'm not bright enough to navigate this new life on autopilot, serious thought must be given.

Leg 1: I get to see my Dad for lunch. Lots of people don't have the luxury (and it is a luxury) of having lunch with their mom or dad. Perhaps a bit of gratitude needed to be reinstated. Leaves less room for that center of the universe thing. So being less enthralled with myself makes me happier. Huh. Great lunch with Dad. He looks awesome and is back to his normal self after a couple of tough years. A hug or two from that guy can fix anything. Oh, and a delicious, calorie free, homemade brownie from Tinker at Manzana's is always a nice travel snack.
Leg 2: Head to Boyne Mountain to celebrate Annette's birthday and hang with my buddy Justin. Rainy, pissy travel but great thinking time. And PERFECT time to crank some tunes.

One of the features of thinking time being the wheel is that you really become in tune with your surroundings and yourself. Meaning that you realize that after several cups of coffee in the morning, a pop on the way to lunch, a couple more cups of coffee AND a bottled water, you find out how bad you have to whiz and exactly how many quality stops there are on Thumb Lake Road... In the old days I probably would have bailed on this leg.

Too far. Too much time driving all over. Too much time away from sitting around drinking a Saturday away. More progress and had a blast with my friends. I was also lucky to see some folks I hadn't seen since my lie came out. More support. Incredible...

Leg 3: The funny part you've been waiting for!

Where a day of thinking about a life better lived interspersed with really fun events came to a head in Boyne City. At a stop light. Here comes the embarrassing part... Raining on and off all day.

Plenty of puddles to nail. One of my favorite pastimes. Finally figured out that autopilot had to be disengaged and I was in a damn fine mood after a great day. Roll into Boyne City and expertly catch a red light. One of two in the whole town.
No big deal. Catching every red light no longer pisses me off. As much. Unless the dickhead that pulled out in front of me and went 40 in a 55 gets through and I get stopped. THAT still pisses me off a bit. Red lights give me a chance to look around and see things I normally wouldn't. Downtown was crazy busy. That little burg has come a long way in the past 10 years.

Sitting behind a minivan at the light. In the rain. Listening to the new Joe Bonamassa release. And people watching and wait a minute... Wow.

Beautiful woman crossing the street with her friends. She was having a blast in the rain while her friends were not.

Quick peek. Typical man thing to do. Light change and off we go. Almost.

See, right in front of that minivan was a jackass that decided to do a U-turn in downtown BC because he saw a parking space on the other side of the street.

Yes, I'm judging him and incredibly accurately at this moment. His super terrific maneuver caused the van in front of me to stop rather suddenly.

Normally not an issue. Except for that last glance to my left to see the pretty girl.

Split second glance mind you, not some drooling, slack jawed stare. Face forward and SLAM on the brakes! Wet pavement + anti-lock brakes = LOTS of noise. I almost nailed that minivan.

All of my "learning" came rushing at me with a minivan rear window full of those cute little family stickers. Dad, mom, three little kids, cat, dog. I could tell that the sticker dog was going to have 5 sticker puppies soon. THAT'S how close I was.

I saw Professor Dickweed make his U-turn in front of the aforementioned minivan and in that split second, made a formerly un-makeable good decision. Instead of yelling and screaming, I laughed.

At myself. And thankfully so.

I looked out my driver's window and saw the pretty lady standing in the middle of the street staring at me. She heard the sliding tires and ALMOST saw a crash. I sheepishly held my hands about a foot apart, gauging how close I was.

She grinned, shook her head and held her fingers about an inch apart. Just missed that van! I did the forehead wipe, she blew me a kiss and the guy driving the minivan tossed his cigarette out the window and flipped me the bird.

I had to accept said bird. Jim "learned" me something Saturday morning. Working the program is just a phrase. To him, it means working the 12 steps of AA. And that is absolutely perfect for him.
To me it means remembering the things that have led to my successes these past few months, remembering the things that I did that caused my failures for those past few years and ACTIVELY choosing how to behave. I'm hoping that someday it will become automatic but I'm not there just yet.

So there you have it.

I'm officially OFF autopilot. Apparently being an active participant in whatever I'm doing is going to keep me from crashing.

I hope they name one of those sticker puppies after me.

16 MY FIRST RADIO INTERVIEW

10.18.16

(fake transcript from a fake interview by a fake DJ on a fake radio station)

DJ Chow: And we're back! Sharing the studio today with a newcomer to the area, Sober Derek! Welcome to the WHAK "Off Color Interview Hour"!

Me: Well thanks Chow, it's an honor to be...

DJ: That's terrific! So how are things going??? Me: Things are going pretty darn well.

DJ: Hey! Watch the language, Mr. Big! This is Off Color not Off The Air!

Me: Umm...sorry? Being a DJ must be difficult. The unique personalities you have to...

DJ: It ain't easy being me, Sober Derek! So this whole quitting drinking thing. Is this some new fad or something? I've been drinking for years and it hasn't affected me. What's the big deal???

Me: Clearly drinking hasn't affected you...

One of the biggest changes is that now when I'm listening to someone talk, I'm not just waiting for them to zip it so I can talk, get it? It's actually fun to listen to people and learn about them.

Seems to be a lot going on even when I'm not involved. Takes some pressure off. Maybe you should try it...

DJ: I'll try anything three or four times, pal! Speaking of that... Time for a WHAK Amole Pizza Muffin Sports Break!

And... it's noon on Tuesday people! There are ZERO scores to report! Time to go to the freezer and grab some pizza muffins for a healthy, gluten free, dairy free, tree nut reduced, GMO enhanced synthetic snack!

Remember, if it tastes like nothing but costs a lot, that's Amole!

Me: Is this really happening?

DJ: You don't mind if I have a quick beer, do ya, sport? This interview is boring with a capital B! Me: Do what you gotta do, son. I have a feeling you will anyway... You sure look familiar...have we met?
DJ: I get that a lot. I'm pretty famous; just ask me, I'll tell you. We both seem to have a face for radio! Just kidding! I'm beautiful! So how long have you been sober?

Me: ...such an asshole...Oh sorry! Well I haven't had a drink in almost 8 months but the recovery status is harder to nail down. A bit more nebulous, if you will. I'm finding that recovery is a state of being that takes constant effort but leaves you much less exhausted. Does that make sense?

DJ: Oh sure it does, buddy! Sounds terrific! What were we talking about? Where's my beer...

Me: Right... So my goal with this book is to bridge the gap between the normals and those in active addiction. Seems like everybody is dealing with something and the things I'm learning in the program seem to work in lots of different ways.

DJ: Work! That reminds me that it's time for the WHAK Jobs report! Hey all you guys over at Pabst that got laid off because this fool, I mean, this gentleman quit drinking, head over to Faygo because he drinks the cherry sparkling water like his guts are on fire! Seriously, you should see this!

Me: I swear we've met before...

DJ: I'd remember you, precious, trust me. I never forget a face. Now where did I put that beer...So do you just sit at home and knit or do those goofy ass adult coloring books? You can't have any of the same friends now that you are a raging quitter.

Me: Actually I am incredibly fortunate. That was one of my biggest concerns and turns out to be one of the biggest reasons I tricked myself into continuing to drink. If I kept drinking and denying that I had a problem, there would be no problem, and life would go merrily on. The flaw in that theory is my closest friends knew I had an issue, I wasn't fooling anyone. I didn't walk down the stairs to "bottom", I jumped out of an airplane with no chute to make sure I punched through bottom. When I came to, my friends and family were right there to help. There was some attrition. An unfortunate consequence of war. Doesn't mean I am giving up. Some of the lost friendships are on life support but I think about them every day and how to help heal them. Not sure that condition is specific to people in active addiction...

DJ: I see... starting to think maybe we HAVE met... Maybe just one more beer...keep talking Mr. Sober...

Me: The quality of my problems had increased dramatically. No more foggy head trying to remember what I "accomplished" the night before. No more wasting days because I'm too tired from lack of actual sleep. A good friend just explained to me Saturday that I have "stabilized."

Not exactly in a position to save the world but at least able to function in a more normal fashion and THINK about helping other people with this stuff some day. It's true that I still think about the exciting peaks and find the smooth "middle" boring but certainly don't miss those self induced lows. Progress. Some exciting projects are in the works that were not possible even six months ago.

DJ: You're trying to tell me that life is perfect without booze. That sounds about as honest as those pizza muffins "healthy snack" claim. What the hell is a pizza muffin anyway? What crazed, almost 8 month no drinking, marketing flunky made that up? It's like he was struggling for a comedic device instead of a wholesome treat...

Me: Life is not perfect by any stretch BUT it is manageable. These new tools I've been given can't fix my time machine or grant me any do-overs. They can however let me stop digging the basement addition to the bottom and start moving forward. My future goal is to help others avoid digging that addition to the bottom. It's dark, dirty, lonely work.

DJ: This pizza muffin is so tasty...

Me: I just figured out where I know you from...

17 THIRSTY DAYS

10.24.16

"On thirsty days just like these, you only get what you can squeeze." - Guy Forsyth in the song – "Mechanic"

"Don't force it Derek, just get a bigger hammer." That's another Dad quote. Sage advice when applied properly. My last two chapters had two weeks between them.

Not because I didn't have anything to say but because I had too much to say. And none of it would have made sense to anyone except for the nutcase writing it. Half a legal pad was sacrificed in the making of that two weeks of silence.

I'm guessing there are some out there offering to buy more legal pads. Why the time out in between chapters? There are a couple reasons.

One, I was in search of a bigger hammer because I was definitely forcing it.

Two, I had coffee with an actual professional after work one night and was reminded that listening was important.

But I want to talk so bad... Being brand spanking new to writing continues to be a learning experience which is incredibly difficult to admit for someone that used to know everything.

Not only is writing a challenge but coming up with topics, entertaining people with said topics while not losing the seriousness of aforementioned topics and avoiding the repetition of certain words is damn near impossible.

How Topics Saved My Life is coming soon to a book store near you... Thirsty days.

Not physical thirst. Mental.

Ever open the fridge and stand there looking for something but not sure what?

Then close the door having not found "it" only to return to not find "it" again? Unless maybe some of you have a different model that has plenty of "it" all the time. If you do, please email me the make and model!

Hold on a sec while I go to the cupboard where the Oreos are supposed to be but aren't because I forgot to grab them when I was buying stupid lettuce and ridiculous fruit. What is the rule about talking to people in the Oreo row???

I'm trying to find something to be super duper happy about! Squeezing the bejeezus out of every event because if you force it, you will find it, right? Another trick played on me by myself?

Example: I like things reasonably neat, tidy, clean, etc. You know, the way they are supposed to be. The wheels on my car were looking pretty shabby. Went to the store, bought the appropriate items and went to work.

First pass and what a change! Missed a few spots though. Not happy. Redo each one. MUCH better. Still a couple spots that aren't QUITE there.

A different brush would help!

Re-spray each wheel and with new brush in hand, get after it.

NOW they are done. Super happy now!

Go inside, have a sandwich and clean my cleaning brushes. So happy! Look at my wheels! So shiny and good and wait, how did I miss that part by the valve stem? Rookie move.

And now I'm pissed because I'm not PERFECTLY happy. The process of forcing myself to be happy was making it worse. Yes, I fixed the part I missed by the valve stem.
The funny part?

My "cottage" has a charming, “natural approach."

That's the realtor way to say “dirt driveway."

It rained like crazy later that night which was awesome for sleeping. Nothing like the sound of rain pounding on the roof of your trailer, I mean cottage.

That same wonderful rain came down hard enough to fill my properly polished wheels full of charming, natural approach aka dirt.

I stayed less than happy about that for a bit until I realized what I was doing to myself. Writing is like cleaning those wheels.

If I regress and don't stay outside of myself, the squeezing begins. Sometimes perfection is simply out of reach and I need to not only realize but accept that. Maybe it's always out of reach but I'm working on the "progress, not perfection" thing at the moment.

I can squeeze a story so hard that the funny part, the message and the therapy that I seek runs right to the editing floor. That doesn't do anybody any good. Remember earlier in the chapter when I was reminded that listening was important?
I listened to my friend's questions.

Why did I feel this compulsion to write? Who was I writing for? Who established the deadline? Why was I making myself so upset about something that didn't need to get done? Did I really think my writing was so important that people would be upset if I didn't hurry up and get one done? Hmm... Squeezing too hard? Do non-addicts obsess over things just like people in active addiction?

Here's my thought... If your wheels aren't perfectly polished does that make them any less round? Can you still roll along and find little bits of happiness here and there?

They were clean, something I could control, until they were dirty, something I couldn't control.

So I did the work, got a positive result, and was upset. Crazy much?

Taking some time away from writing, rolling around on my mostly clean wheels and being thankful for progress, not perfection, somehow made writing fun and easy again.

Not sure if this chapter was worth reading or not but it was worth writing. I'm sure it will rain and dirt will splash up but there is polish under that dirt now, making cleaning much easier.

And it will rain in life.

The dirt will splash up on us but now we know if we properly "polish" our mind, body and spirit, it won't stick and will rinse right down the gutter where it belongs.

18 DON'T THROW AWAY YOUR MOW-MOW

10.31.16

I was looking through pictures of my kids when they were tiny. When they were babies. They both learned to walk early. They also both had the assistance of the Fisher Price Activity Walker. This little folding gem was a wheeled tripod of mobility.

It also had spinners and mirrors and a phone dial for when the commute across the living room was too exhausting. It seemed a little pretentious to say, "Let's grab your Activity Walker" so we shortened it to "mow-mow". It was actually short for "mower." It'll make more sense later in the chapter. Eight months ago I decided to give up. No more booze. Ever again. Back in that cold, dark, shitty February, "ever again" didn't seem that long.

Thankfully today, it seems like forever, and that is a wonderful feeling. One day at a time for the rest of my life. There are days that theory feels a bit daunting.

There are even MOMENTS that force one to reflect on how long forever really is and if it is truly worth it. The correct answer is yes.

We humans spend our lives striving for success in one form or another. We learn to crawl so we can walk. We learn to walk so we can run. We learn to run so we can get away from the cops.

I'm just kidding! Mostly. Just seeing if you were still with me. One of the things that I'm learning as I start to walk in my new life is that I kind of gave crawling the finger.

Crawling is an important step in life and recovery. The fall from a crawl isn't as damaging or painful as one from a dead run down the side of that gravel pit.

The problem with crawling is that it is S L O W... Once we decide that enough is enough, it's time to get on with the show and fix it. All of it, all at once.

A little hurry up wouldn't kill ya, would it??? Ever been given a task at work that you really wanted and you were just so excited and you were going to get it done so fast and so well and so under budget and, and, and... you blow it. You fall flat on your face. Same type of deal with this new project the boss gave me.

Only now I'm the boss. Of myself. The nice part about the human condition is somewhere in the back of the mind, in parts we can't consciously access, we don't want to give up. I really believe that.

Every single one of you faithful readers has taken on a project and struggled. I'm talking struggled with a capital "uggled."

Maybe you just tossed it aside and said the hell with it.

Wasn't worth doing anyway. Too damn busy to screw with it right now. I know those are all possible excuses because some guy told me. What happens to that stupid project that allegedly wasn't worth our attention to begin with? It sits there.

Oh, and we subconsciously continue to think about how to complete it. Compelled to succeed. What's wrong with that, you ask?

Read on and we can answer that and figure out how that little activity walker gadget fits in! So what is so wrong with that compulsion to succeed?

My untrained opinion is that we aren't trained to fall. Not so dangerous when we are learning to crawl but there can be some pain when learning to walk. Enter the activity walker made by a company that has entertained children for decades.

The company has no idea that said walker reminds little ones of a push mower thus the more accurate name, "mow-mow."

Both of my kids transitioned from crawling to walking with the help of a mow-mow.

Here's the exact routine: stand them up, have them grab the mow-mow by the handlebars, point them at mom and it's off to the races. Mom re-aims them to dad and off they go again.

Much fun was had by all! Until the little shits figured out how to get up to the handlebars by themselves... The go like hell was still there but if mom or dad wasn't there to re-aim them, let's just say the noise you heard wasn't joyous laughter. 99 times out of 100 the little ones weren't hurt.

100 times out of 100 they were displeased that the mow-mow was not aimed in the right direction. Soon enough, the mow-

mow wasn't needed for walking and those beautiful babies were walking around on their own.

Now open doors, stairs and other hazards had to be guarded against. The transition from crawling to walking was exciting and nerve wracking for mom and dad as well as the littles.
I bet you are wondering what a mow-mow has to do with sobriety.

Only everything! AA is my sobriety mow-mow. Putting down the bottle was the transition from laying flat on my back to crawling.

I suppose that could be taken literally and figuratively. Big first step?

Whoa boy. How many times does an infant try to roll over before they get it and how hard are their little minds and bodies working?

Exhausting just watching them. You can see the sense of accomplishment in their little faces and YOU know it is just the beginning.

Extrapolate that. Getting through the first ninety days was that transition from crawling to having my hands put on that proverbial mow-mow.

Physically stronger, mentally a tick better but nowhere near ready to walk on my own. Reading the things that I wrote in my journal those first 90 days prove that I truly was just thawing out.

The *Old Timers* were watching, hoping to see me at the next meeting. Come on kid, keep coming back. Push that mow-mow back to another meeting.

You can do it. We will charge you up, send you back to the outside world and hope like hell you come back.

Call anytime. Guess what I did? I called anytime. Pointed my virtual mow-mow back to a meeting as soon as I could and motored for all I was worth!

Sometimes two or three times a day!

I just got my eight month token. Lots of people, including me some days, never thought I'd make it this far. I didn't put a man on the moon or solve world hunger but it's still a pretty cool accomplishment.

The PROBLEM is that now that I have a few months of "walking" behind me, I'm ready to run, right?

No. No, I'm not. And I was reminded of that. The character flaw of arrogance rears its head. Oddly enough, I'm now in meetings about my meetings. My fearless leader (I don't want him to know he's an Old Timer) has graciously offered to burn the remainder of his Saturday mornings on a few of us that need/want "extra credit."

A relapse prevention plan (learning to fall so I don't) is now in place. Cue the mental picture of that beautiful mow-mow.

I'm not ready to run yet.

Hell, that mow-mow is closer to hand than it's been in quite some time. Walking is good for those of us in early recovery. Physically and mentally. And I'm OK with that.

19 BUT AM I A PRETTY ROCK?

11.08.16

This chapter is going to be a challenge to write but hopefully not a challenge to read. A friend asked me to write about "acceptance."

Acceptance is something we should all work on a bunch. It's key to our survival. It's important enough to be a part of the Serenity Prayer so that tells me something.

Things have been going very well lately. Some challenges that I was concerned with never actually materialized.

Some REALLY nice surprises dealing with the book have popped up. My first official speaking engagement for 2017 is on the books for crying out loud! When is something bad going to happen??? The answer is "someday" BUT I no longer have to live in dread. I've learned something pretty cool thanks to the extra credit work assigned to me by my friend Scott.

Ready? We have to accept GOOD things just as well as bad things. I gave that statement its own line because I believe it's that important.

Good things happen! Sometimes we have to look a little harder but they are definitely there.

I don't think that applies solely to those of us that are in recovery so... Commitment to topic made, off I go in search of inspiration.

How hard can it be to get inspired about acceptance? It's a cornerstone of recovery and after taking some time to honestly think about some of the happiest people I know, it's pretty important to normals as well.

Unfortunately, it seems the more frivolous the topic, the easier it is to write about.

What to do... Back to the well of inspiration! Walk down the steps to the lake and wow. It's gorgeous.

The water was so calm and the colors blended so well that you could barely tell where the lake ended and the sky began. Not hard to get lost in thought.

Lost enough to plunk down on my rock and drain the brain. Yes, it looked like I tipped over a thimble of water as opposed to dumping out a five gallon bucket, smarty pants! Not sure if it's meditation or just plain old daydreaming but it worked.

Oh I didn't find inspiration but did I find peace? A Great Lake full of it!

Now what? Now I walk back up the stairs and hope to find this great inspiration elsewhere.

My beach is pure rock. Not a grain of sand to be found. Trust me, if there was one, it would have found its way into my flip flop by now.

So annoying... Navigating this rocky beach requires one to look down to avoid falling on one's ass. I failed at finding inspiration; maybe I can avoid wiping out and in the process, find a cool rock for my friend Nancy's collection! Yeah, see, the bulk of the rocks on my beach are super boring. Flat, tan colored, boring ass rocks.

What do you do with boring ass rocks? Throw them into the lake whence they came!

How many of us have spent countless hours skipping stones, throwing for distance or just going for the biggest splash? Is THAT meditation?

Not sure but I was enjoying mindlessly tossing those boring ass rocks. Then I found a nice "roundy" that I could really get out there. A quick toss in the air, a quick glance at the little bugger, a firm grip and send it! And the split second that it left my hand, I realized I just sent a nice Petoskey stone out into the deep.

By "the deep" I mean it probably only traveled 20 feet (I'm no Verlander) but still well beyond wading depth. That could have been Nancy's rock, dammit! Hell with it, I'm going to go up, make dinner and listen to some new tunes.

Bye rocks! Enjoy your boring ass selves! I've accepted that I'm STILL uninspired AND lousy at picking pretty rocks. OR... Am I quitter that hurled his peace into the lake like a boring ass rock (or Petoskey stone, dammit)?

An important part of this whole "new life" thing is actually following through on the lessons I'm learning, not just reading them and checking them off some imaginary list.

Did I really believe that there was not one super cool rock on that entire beach? (Actually I kind of did but that doesn't fit the story so pretend I didn't.) Heck no! Back down the stairs and about 5'9" away (give or take) was a gorgeous red and black rock.

I'm no rockologist but I am guessing you would be very proud to have this gem in your rock collection. What REALLY happened here?

From a boring ass rock's perspective, a lot. Rock was laying on the beach, enjoying a gorgeous fall afternoon in total peace. An outside force completely changed everything that rock was experiencing. Guess what that rock is going to do? Ride the waves back to shore and have great stories to tell his new rock pals. Not part of his original plan but true acceptance allows for some amazing gifts. From my perspective, also a lot. I was so excited that someone liked my writing enough to request a topic that I was going to knock it out of the park.

It was going to be super duper and it was going to be ready to deliver on Monday (today is Tuesday) and she was going to feel better. Mind you, she simply requested a topic, not a due date. Now the chapter is late (no it isn't) and I'm stressed to the max (no I'm not). Here's what I learned about acceptance so far. Inside forces have just as much or more influence on our serenity as outside forces. The difference is we can get a jump on accepting the inside stuff because WE create it!

I had total peace sitting down at that beach but temporarily tossed it out because I'm not conditioned to accept the good stuff. Yet. Did someone in the audience just whisper, "Balance"?

Problem solvers have a much easier time accepting chaos because we can focus on fixing it.

Accepting gifts?

Not so much. There's still lots of work to do, but once again, getting outside of one's self is necessary and oddly effective.

Marsy, I hope you like your chapter. Nancy, I hope you like your rock.

Thank you *both* for teaching me something without even trying.

20 WHAT POWER YOU HAVE

12.04.16

I just figured out why writing a book takes so long.
It's actually hard work and takes a ton of time.

Unless that's all one does for a living, other stuff gets in the way. Why didn't someone tell me this?!?!

Enough whining.

Time to get to work on this chapter. This is the first one I'm writing with the assistance of my new glasses and I have to say I hate how clear all these little letters are...seems ironic to be writing about superpowers while wearing glasses but that is a totally different story.
Maybe that one will be about denial... Ok, NOW enough whining.

Hi everyone!

Good to be back.

I've really missed interacting with you.

One of my character flaws is the ability to take people for granted and this extended time between chapters made me realize how important you all are to me so, thank you!

For what, you ask?

For sharing your superpowers with me, *of course!*

Let me explain... A LONG time ago, I was in first grade.

Ma packed me and half-pint lunches and Pa told us we'd best skedaddle because we had the coal for our one room schoolhouse and winter was fixin' to set in but good this day!

Slight exaggeration and *poor English on purpose* but it has been quite some time since I was in first grade. Mom packed a lunch for me in my sweet, Superman lunchbox complete with matching thermos.

Big surprise, huh? Back in the olden days, we didn't carry backpacks to first grade. We didn't exactly carry a slate and books wrapped in a strap but a lunchbox was standard equipment. Getting off the bus and into class was priority one. Mrs. Romanik was a great teacher but VERY strict.

Haste makes waste but don't be late. I step down from bus 77-D and head into the hallowed halls of Wilson Elementary School and the latch on my trusty lunchbox proved to be less than trustworthy.

Apparently, those old metal lunch boxes had a spring loaded mechanism that activated when the latch was thrown while in vertical position because shit went everywhere, immediately.

Not smart enough to be embarrassed or hungry enough to care about my lunch; my focus was on the matching Superman thermos.

This was a day that I realized that people *other than Mom and Dad* had superpowers.

My friend Becky S. (remember how our last names only had one letter back then?) stopped and helped me gather all my stuff up and get it put back together.

I didn't ask for help and she didn't ask for or expect a cookie payment, she just got to work. I can't remember my phone number these days but I will never forget that act. Becky S. has superpowers.

Ironically, the "classroom" I'm in now has students with one-letter last names but their superpowers are no less apparent. Thoughtful reflection is such a powerful learning tool. Fast forward past the one-room schoolhouse of yore to modern day.

The time spent reflecting forced me to think about whether or not we all have superpowers.

The best answer I can come up with is, "I think so?" Some will call it energy or power or mojo or juju but I think we all have some good "stuff" inside.

The people in the program, especially the *Old Timers*, have great powers and have learned to use them judiciously and more often than not, only when asked. Sometimes, my enthusiasm makes me want to use my powers instantly and to their full extent.

I liken it to getting a kitten out of a tree for a sweet old lady but in our hurry to rescue the kitten we shove sweet granny out of the way and in the process she breaks a hip.

Best intentions, kitty is out of the tree but grandma now walks with a serious limp.

My experience in recovery is only 9 months old but it seems like the people that are truly "in" have a vested interest in seeing everyone succeed.

I think that you normals of the good-guy persuasion are the same. You like to see others succeed and it's easy to lend a hand, asked or not.

My goal with this book is to share the shareable from the program with you normals. The commitment to everyone succeeding is 100%.

So many of you are helping others succeed and don't even realize it. Being able to step back and watch you unorganized, non-step following, no meeting attending, goofballs helping each other is so damn cool! Using your superpowers for good and you clearly have no idea what you are doing. So cute!

The Christmas season is upon us and though joyous for some, it's a time of strife for others. Sometimes using your superpowers in a way that you normally wouldn't is the right thing to do and you may make someone's day or even year.

Sometimes a knowing wink or understanding smile is super enough. We never know what struggles the other person is dealing with so let's do our best to help people pick up their figurative thermoses.

Thanks for showing me that superpower way back when, Becky S!

Wilson Elementary School Wildcats rule!

21 WHEN HEROES FALL

12.13.16

If you are looking for the Christmas special that leaves you feeling like a Norman Rockwell painting, you may want to wait for next week's episode.

I was told that one has to write the ugly to make room for the beautiful so I'm going to make that room. Growing up, I was fortunate enough to have many heroes. Some real, some imaginary.

For those of you that have read some of my stuff, you might be able to pick out a certain comic book superhero that stands for truth, justice and the American way. He's a bit obscure but I think he's going to be a big deal someday so keep your eyes peeled...
This chapter is going to require some reader participation but don't worry, it won't be graded.

I need your help to make this chapter effective. I need you to close your eyes and picture your real life hero.

When did you meet? What about them makes them hero material? Are they the strong, silent type? Are they gregarious? Was there a life changing event that elevated them to hero status or was it a slow process of building taller and taller pedestals to place them on?

This is important so please, take your time. Got your person? Remember how they rose to the top?

Good deal. Here we go. I try to set a goal for each chapter. One for you and one for me.

This time you get two goals.

First, I hope you reaffirm your faith in your hero.

Second, I hope you realize that you are a hero to someone and more likely than not, many "someones."

I have the best readers so you obviously have more people calling you heroes, right? The goal I set for myself is to get some more of my "ugly" out to make room for the "beautiful."

I was once a hero to someone very important to me. I'm not a hero anymore.
It hurt to receive that message. The pedestal had been crumbling for a few years but I decided to jump from what altitude I had left into a bottle. The problem with the bottle I chose is that its bottom was much farther down than I imagined.

Some people seek out hero status and some shun it. I don't think I sought it out in the beginning but toward the end, I clung to it.

I did so because in my mind, it was one of the few things that couldn't be taken away from me and I was right. It wasn't taken from me, I threw it away of my own volition. Pride, arrogance and self loathing made sure of it.

One of the many things I've learned about my condition is that those afflicted will justify damn near anything in order to keep drinking.

We also know, perhaps subconsciously, that it is an unsustainable way to live. We won't admit it but we know the end of our run is coming.

The run could be a job, a relationship, our physical and/or mental health, our hero status or our lives. It could be all of the above and for me, almost was.

Surrounded by tons of loving friends and family and all I could think about was what was going to happen to ME once my lie came out.

Never mind how THEY were going to feel. If I kept drinking, I could quiet my insane brain, smother the flames of impending doom and retain my hero status just a little longer. Normal people don't act like that, people in active addiction do. I told the lie and like every single lie ever told in the history of lying, the truth came out.

Family embarrassed, friendships ended, hero status removed. One fell swoop.

There was no recovering from what I had done and I was certain of it. Except recovery is exactly what was needed. Recovery is allowing me to live two lives in one lifetime. Don't squander that second life, right? February 2016 was the bottom.

It was a hard bottom, too. The collateral damage was extensive. I've seen my son once since I've been sober and my daughter, not at all.

These past almost ten months have been emotionally exhausting. From almost not being here to write this to actually looking forward to each day is quite the miracle and I need to remind myself of that from time to time. Thank you to each and every one of you.

Thank you for being heroes to me. There have been some incredibly tough moments but somehow, YOU found the strength to stick around.

You lead by example without knowing. That's hero type stuff. Now, the rest of your assignment. Get in touch with YOUR hero. As you all know, "heroing" is hard work and they would probably love to hear from you, no matter how you need to communicate.

And I know you know what I mean.

22 SEEK THE MESSAGE, NOT THE MESS

12.25.16

It's Christmas morning at the Cottage of Solitude. This is the first Christmas in my life that I woke up to a completely empty house. No significant other, no family, and for the first time since she was born, no little girl. She is safe and sound and happy with her mom and I'm guessing still sleeping as I write this.

The excitement of trying to find perfect gifts for other people didn't happen this year. Dad is in sunny Florida and Mom and little sister are in Colorado.
My go-to friends are scattered from Florida to the Carolinas to Ohio to California. I have been dreading this morning, to be sure. Being the de facto Santa for years, I knew the tree wouldn't be surrounded with presents. See any reasons for me to drink?

Happily, me neither. And after that heartbreaking start to my morning, I saw that I was completely wrong about the tree being bereft of gifts. It's absolutely full! Any chance you would sit with me for a bit while I open them?

I have eggnog. And cookies.

So many cookies...

Any self respecting present un-wrapper would go for the biggest one first so I'm doing the same! I used to prank the kids by putting something small in a big box so I hope it hasn't happened to me...

Sound of wrapping paper being shredded...

Boy...that is a lot of tape...

Who uses this much tape!!!

Oh come on!!!

Even pretend presents have to mess with me???

It's like Ft. Knox only with tape!!!

OK, it's open. And it's a piece of paper. Too small to be a check with a huge sum written on it.

It's a handwritten note.

"You don't have to drink today."

Wow. That is EXACTLY the right size box because this gift is huge!

I don't have to drink today.

Of any of the above sad conditions I woke up to, which would be made better by adding booze?

Not a single one.

You normals might struggle with this, but a few short months ago, any single one of those sad thoughts would have been more than enough to justify adding rum to this eggnog.

Nice to be beyond that.

Thank you, Mystery Gift Giver!!!

Maybe ease up on the tape?

Save a tape tree? Ooohhh!

The next "gift" I go to unwrap has Superman wrapping paper!!! Appears to be minimal tape.

Open time! *(I'm being a bit more careful with the unwrapping business this time as I am the one that has to take care of the scraps of paper so...)*

It's an email...

"I wouldn't want it any other way. :)

That is a response to an amends and a thank you to one of my best friends that I've known since I was just a wee shaver.

(for the record, I've been shaving since I was about 5 so...)

Unfortunately this person saw me during my last few days of drinking.

It was ugly. I was ugly.

Embarrassing.
Humiliating.

This present is an excellent reminder of how bad things were but how good things can be.
This present makes my prescription glasses fill up with water or something so I'm going to just hang it on my tree *(yes, it's a magic Christmas tree so I can hang emails on it)*
It's what I've always wanted (and now realize what I've always had) so thank you!

This one is shaped like a DVD or something. It's wrapped perfectly.

It's almost too pretty to open.

Not anymore!!! Boom!
(all scraps are properly placed in the bag for recycling so please don't worry about a mess forming)

It's a necklace.

Umm... anyone that knows me very well at all knows my thoughts on necklaces.

(Never trust a man that owns more than zero necklaces. My thoughts.)

It's a pendant of St. Jude, patron saint of lost causes.

The reason it was in a round package is because the pendant is from one of my all-time favorite movies, "Man on Fire."

It may not be a necklace much longer.
(like right now, it's a good luck charm, the necklace part is no longer with us)
Some people have such impressive memories. This little charm will travel with me for the rest of my days. After that, someone else can take care of it.
I can feel the power in this little piece of metal and it needs to be shared.

Someday. This one is wrapped a little wonky and it's a bit squishy... Socks.

Who's the joker that got me hypothetical socks??? Right in the middle of all the serious gifts!

Real funny...socks...pfft...

These three little boxes are all tied together. Beautifully wrapped.

Blue, green and red foil paper with matching bows. The Christmas lights are reflecting off each one. Absolutely breathtaking.

Not anymore!!!! This wrapping paper just disappears when I tear it off. Hmm... Gratitude, humility and serenity. Wow.

No wonder these three boxes were tied together. These are gifts I was promised if I worked my program.

It seems like if I don't pay close attention to one of them, the remaining two start to fade. So some smarty pants gave me gifts that require work? The best things in life require effort. That effort can be your time. Maybe your appreciation. Someone out there is pulling for you to succeed.

Reward them by putting in the time and succeeding. It's fun to make people happy.

This last one is wrapped in plain brown paper. Looks kind of like the mailman was a bit upset about having to deliver this one.

Hope it wasn't fragile.

I'm going to open this one carefully.
Might even save the paper. Shit. It was fragile. The damage wasn't done by the mailman, it was done by me. The gift is the love of my friends and family and it's beat up a bit. It's not totally shattered but it's definitely damaged.

I don't think they make the kind of tape I need to put all of this back together the way it was before I forgot what a precious gift it truly is.

The reason the wrapping paper is so worn is because I open this gift numerous times every day.

The good news is I'm working with a new kind of tape now. *The "scotch" tape is gone for good.* The label on this new stuff says "recovery" and this stuff holds things together like nothing I've ever tried before.

A Christmas miracle that started back in February and continues to happen every day.
Well I think that about does it for gift opening. Amazing treasures under this little tree! What could've turned into a real disaster of a day has turned into a miracle. I can be sad for a bit and that is OK now.

It will pass and do so much easier than days gone by when I

added copious amounts of "medicine."

The *Old Timers* told me in order to keep my gift of recovery, I had to give it away. At first, that sounded ridiculous. Everything around me was a giant mess because of what I had done.

I was going to keep that for myself and never let go!

Now I get the message and hope to be able to give it just as well!

It has been an amazing ten months and there is no way I can ever repay you all for the love and support.

I'll keep working hard and we can see where this adventure takes us.

Merry Christmas!

23 TRACTION IS PRECIOUS

1.11.17

Happy New Year! 2017 is upon us and I think it has plenty of good things in store! Apparently dumping snow on a daily basis is top priority for whoever controls the weather and their goal is being met with a great deal of success...

First chapter of the new year.

What a year 2016 was.

One for the ages, without question. Finally determined that I wasn't quite as good at drinking as I thought so I gave it up on February 23, 2016 and have been working to get and stay sober ever since.
Quite the adventure. The amount of learning coupled with the support of some known and some previously unknown well wishers has led to a great new way of thinking and ultimately, living.

Good people want to see people succeed and being surrounded by so many good people proves that on a daily basis. THANK

YOU ALL!!!!

There is the mushy stuff. Now let's get to the business of explaining that chapter title and why traction is so precious.

The title is something my Dad said to me back in the car racing days. Some of my favorite memories come from the year we raced against each other.

Little did I know that life lessons were being taught and learned while having fun racing with and against Dad.

Short track racing is an aggressive sport that requires an incredibly light touch, finesse, strategy, patience and horsepower.

Lots and lots of delicious horsepower.

Dad made sure the engine he built for my car had horsepower to spare, I just had to come up with all the other stuff. On the job training at race pace!

One particularly hot summer day, we were at the track early, practicing and working on our car setups.
85 and sunny. No breeze.

Wearing a Nomex fire suit and full-face helmet while strapped in to a black and red race car with a boiling hot engine at my feet and the exhaust running inches from my right side.

Hell yes it's fun! Never kept track of how many pounds of water weight we lost each race but it was substantial. Out on the track we go.

Always 5 to 10 warm up laps to get engine and tires up to temp then it's literally off to the races. My car would usually turn better than Dad's but he could get on the gas sooner.

Made for some great but frustrating dog fights!

This day, my car wouldn't let me get on the gas OR turn.

We did our practice laps and headed for the pits. We were both hot but one of us was pissed right off. I'm guessing that there were probably other things on my mind but memory fails me.

"What was wrong out there? Why weren't you keeping up?", said Dad. "I'm guessing it's because I am driving the piece of shit old car and you are driving the brand new one you had built specifically for this track," said idiot son. "Nothing to do with the loose nut behind the wheel?" said Dad.

"@#$&%* and $#&%* and *%$&#@$&..." said idiot son.

Smiling, Dad pulled me aside, away from the crew. A quick lesson ensued.

"You are hot, your car is hot and the track is hotter. Your engine is coming on the power curve at a different rpm than you are used to because of the temp and humidity.

Your tires are boiling tread off every lap because the more angry you get, the more you abuse them. Based on your driving style, you will be buying new tires before the night is out."

"Traction is precious."

"It's your best friend out there. You can't turn without it and you certainly can't use the horsepower you have. Right now it's bad, do you think is going to get easier when all the other cars are fighting for the exact same spot you want? Lots of adjustments can be made on that "old piece of shit" that you are driving for fun. Want some help?"

Jeeze, Dad.

When do I get to stop learning and just "know stuff" like him...?

What the heck does that story have to do with sobriety? Racing cars is surely not the best activity for serenity seekers. Peace be with you while I pass you on the inside and leave a bit of my paint for you to remember this moment by... Coming off a years long bender, my "tires" were shot.

The track of life was hotter than I'd ever experienced. I wasn't concerned with finessing my way back on track; I was just using horsepower to push my way through. The problem with that style of "racing" is that I almost hit the wall so hard that I couldn't walk away from the crash.

It wasn't a sustainable way to live. Now my "pit-crew" consists not only of friends and family, but the people of my recovery community.

Now I am constantly making adjustments to my "chassis" so I can steer better. I am getting more adept at applying throttle when I feel traction.

Not that I don't spin my tires from time to time, but it's easier to judge it now.

If my car is turning into that "old piece of shit" I can pull into the pits of any number of places that support recovery and there is a crew of experts *(Old Timers)* ready and willing to help, whether it's fine tuning or starting from baseline setup of "one day at a time."

There are still people that are competing for the same spot and

that's OK. Some are people that want help and some are just jerks.
It's fun "racing" with the people that want help, they push me to focus and be a better driver. Now when you feel a bump just before we enter the turn, it's just me tapping your back bumper letting you know I'm there, not trying to power you out of the way.

Traction IS precious.

24 A LOW DOWN SHAKIN' CHILL

02.15.17

Son House wrote a song called "Walkin' Blues" and said, "The blues ain't nothin' but a low-down shakin' chill."

Ever been so sick that you've got every blanket in the house piled on top of yourself (plus that little blue kitchen towel with a sailboat embroidered on it because your mom sent it to you) and you STILL can't get warm? Shivering as you are burning up with fever and freezing to death at the same time?

Can you physically feel that if you think about it hard enough? Excellent!
Let's explore what "feelings" feel like to a thawing ex-boozer. I never took the time to think about feelings before I started this adventure. My professional opinion is that I equated feelings with weakness or vulnerability.

If a person showed sadness, they were weak.

If they showed anger, they lacked control.

If they showed fear or trepidation, they were vulnerable. If they showed happiness, they were hiding something.

These keen observations weren't the result of my upbringing, quite the opposite.

My parents always taught my sister and I to talk about stuff and that it was OK to show emotion, good and bad. Just because they taught me that stuff doesn't mean I applied it.

Alcohol was not only something I enjoyed the many flavors of, it was a useful and ahem... much needed tool. Booze was the sandpaper to the sharp edges of feelings. Round 'em off a bit and they don't cause so many issues.

Ever hear the saying, "Just a quick one to take the edge off"? It's because we mean exactly that. For some reason, addicts are simply not wired for the intensities of feelings.

Emotional fuses blow. Going through my journal shows how the feeling "amp" started to come back to life. I'm in my forties so my "feeling amp" is tube type and yes, it takes a bit to warm up.

Flicking the power switch to "On" and all I hear is crackling and an all too familiar hiss...and it's loud... fear.

What are people going to say now that they know about my lie? Is that person looking at me funny? Was that guy a bit standoffish?

Imagine looking at your friends and having to wonder if they were still your friends.

Why the first feeling I had couldn't have been elation or relief is beyond me.

Maybe it's because as we peel the onion, the ugly stuff is closest to the surface. I hated going places.

The center of the universe thinking that is inherent in alcoholics leads to a powerful case of paranoia.

I was immersed in this new experiment and assumed everyone knew and was talking about it and me.

A few might have been, most could've cared less. Another drunk proclaiming he is changing his ways. Big deal. Lots of snapping and crackling going on in those early days. Hoping for the best and unable to prepare for the worst. But the amp started to warm up...

The snapping and crackling and hissing started to fade, or more likely was overrun, by the loud screeching sound of feedback... anger and resentment.

So much louder than fear. Why didn't someone tell me what was happening??? Why didn't one of my people tell me to put the bottle down???

You said you loved me yet you watched me dig deeper and deeper! Oh, now you want to judge me?!?!

What are you looking at??? It wasn't my fault!!! The snapping and crackling and hissing is coming back intermittently and the feedback is on full blast.

The normal fix would have been to wipe the tubes down with alcohol. Clean things up a bit.

Fortunately, I was lucky enough to have a repair shop full of fellow "musicians" to help me keep adjusting things instead of shit-canning the amp I had.

Unfortunately, searching for that perfect tone takes time. At this point, all I could "hear" was loud noise. Going from “not feeling” to “feeling” these things SUCKED!

It's no wonder some give up. The search for tone is not for the weak of heart. The important thing to keep in mind is that there is a bunch of experienced tuners ready and willing to help anytime.

All kinds of all racket happening and what's this? What is that echoing sound?

Reverb. Amp work is incredibly exhausting.

The body is starting to heal but the brain is still in shock. So many new noises and suddenly there is way too much reverb.

Echoes of the past.

Joy and happiness.

Guilt and sadness.

Fond memories pop into your head like a favorite song then someone drags the needle across the entire record as though you will never get those times back.

The good memories hurt more than the bad ones... That low-down shakin' chill of the blues?

It's here with a vengeance. The brain is an amazing machine but it can be a heartless bastard and there isn't a damn thing you can do about it.

This is when we realize that in reality, it isn't anyone else's fault. WE caused the ruined recording sessions. You look in your recording studio and you see the priceless guitars (relationships) smashed beyond repair.

The drum kit that your mom and dad bought you for Christmas (career) is kicked in and thrown around. Your entire case of harmonicas (happiness) is missing without a trace.

I'm not sure if any of you have ever been so blue that your heart physically hurt but I got there. It's painful. And this is AFTER I quit drinking! Something compelling kept happening.

The boys in the band always said the same thing after each "jam session". "Keep coming back." So I did. And just like they promised, things started sounding better! The snapping and crackling and hissing faded. Feedback? Always a potential but now I know what causes it and more importantly, how to remedy it.

Reverb? A very good part of your song, in moderation. Those old records aren't broken or ruined by scratches. You can still play them and feel the good feels. Right now my amp is running better than it has in many, many years.

If I look inside, the tubes are glowing a beautiful blue-orange glow.

You can see the curls in the filaments as clear as day and feel the warmth rolling out.

The control knobs are balanced for the tune I'm playing now. Not too bright or tinny with treble, not too booming or muffled by bass.
The song I'm working on right now is called "Feelings are Normal" and it sounds pretty good through this rebuilt amp.

I'm going to keep going back to the shop to find the perfect tone because the *Old Timers* know stuff I don't. Maybe I'll crank my happiness volume up a bit, too.

Rock on, people...

25 STAY STURDY

03.21.17

It has been quite some time since I've written anything and I actually have reasons, not excuses. Lots of effort was required to get up to and get through my one year anniversary.

The pressure we place on ourselves is far more intense than anything an outsider could ever aspire to. The desire to drink didn't surface but I definitely could feel some of the old ways of thinking working their way to the surface.

Trying to manage the excitement of actually making it a whole year and prepping for the anticlimactic letdown of day 366 was incredibly challenging. I'm damn near to thirteen months so I think it's safe to write again.

I'm rusty and have been fighting with two potential topics so I flipped a coin and this is the one that I start year two with. I saw an old transport cart at work one day and it fascinated me.

There are probably a dozen or so of them rolling around. The carts have been around for decades. Some of the people that have worked there awhile guessed the carts have been around 50 years or more.

Not sure why I was so taken with this particular model but I'm going to try and explain it to myself and in turn, maybe you as well.

I think the reason this chapter has been so vexing is that it is just another analogy but it's one that helps me figure out roles and relationships.

How things work together. Let's start with the floor of the factory. I see the floor as life.

It wouldn't matter how masterfully built your cart was, if it didn't have something to roll on, it would be useless.

The challenge I've been working on is accepting that the floor my cart is rolling on isn't perfectly polished and smooth.

I've also realized that although our carts may be different, we are all sharing the same floor. The trick is to be mindful of the fact that this huge floor has infinite characteristics and we are all rolling over different spots, all the time. Some are jostling over the cracks of a broken heart while others are gliding across the freshly polished marble of new love.

Some are stuck in a damaged section of anxiety and sorrow while others cruise smoothly across serenity and joy. Some of us had to fishtail out of control, through something that spilled...

Now for the wheels. The steel wheels on this cart are decorative AND functional.

The builder could have used plain ole' spokes but chose not to and I think that was on purpose.

I think the wheel is our heart.

The emotions one, not the pumping one.

The ornate design is what people see.

At least what we think they see.

The edges of the wheels are beat up and even though we want to believe people only see the intricate design, eventually, the miles of abuse start to show.

It's impossible to hide. What I'm learning and hoping to share is that the miles are ok to see.

They are just as much a part of our wheel, if not more, than the pretty parts.
The dings and dents, the rust and chipped paint. All are parts of our wheel and if looked at from proper perspective, even more beautiful than the design we wanted people to see.

I never dreamed I would become an old wheel but I did and now I know it's ok.

No longer rolling through the booze has removed the rust from the wheels.

The path across the floor of recovery isn't perfectly smooth and sometimes it's bumpier than the rum soaked floor I used to roll across.

Some of those bumps are by design and while frustrating, they are necessary.

They are built in to shake the big pieces of rust and buildup loose so that eventually, you can start the polishing process.

Making a difficult apology removes the ugly rust but can leave a ding.

Dings can be smoothed over time but rust tends to build up and get uglier as that time passes. Dings are better than rust.

The polishing part can be as simple as pausing to watch a sunset, noticing how many stars are actually in the sky, smiling at a stranger in the grocery store or as intricate as planning a fun date to spoil someone you care about. Options begin to present themselves without even looking.

Now for the decking.

This is a tough part to write.

This whole chapter has been a challenge for almost a month but this part really made me think.

The decking is your friends, family and in my case, my recovery.

The wheels may never get a break but they are steel and are built for some of the self inflicted damage.

The boards that make up the deck are sturdy and your cart would be useless without them but they take a beating.

The hardest thing to come to terms with is that the beating they took because of me.

That stings.

The shame, regret and embarrassment can be overwhelming.

The things I have thrown on my deck have been incredibly damaging.

Some of the boards are completely shattered and can't be repaired.

Some of them are damaged but if patiently tended to, they can be fixed.

Some of the boards are pure miracles. I decided to roll my cart off the floor straight into a car crusher. Some of the boards held.
Mom and Dad.

My friends.

People I didn't even know.

Damage was done, no question, but they held.

I found out that some were actually holding each other together.
I'm not dropping the sharp cornered, ten ton lies on my deck anymore.

No more dumping gallons of toxic behavior on it either. Nope, in order for that sturdy cart to stay sturdy, all of it needs to be cared for.

It's important to remember that maintenance is much easier than repair.
I've recently been introduced to a new maintenance technique called "sharing my thoughts."

I'm beta testing it right now and will keep you posted if this new age voodoo actually works.
There. The cart experiment is finally done.

If you want a picture of the cart that inspired this chapter, sign up for the newsletter at derekchowen.com.

Thanks for bearing with me on this one. It's clunky because I am out of practice and for that, I apologize.

Maybe this will help shake a piece of rust loose or polish things a bit.

You are all a big part of my decking and I really appreciate you.

Stay Sturdy!

26 SERENITY INTERRUPTED

06.26.17

It was a dark and stormy night... This time it actually fits! This story doesn't start that way but let me tell you, it works its way up to it! Sometimes the trick with writing is figuring out where to start, how much back-story to include and how much detail to overwhelm you with.

My thought process is, "do I lose you in the beginning or have you put it down wondering why you spent the time in the first place."

A delicate balance, to be sure. I went on a sailing adventure. Been working between 60 and 70 hours a week so a little break was earned.

The hours are the main reasons I haven't been writing. Or going out for dinner. Or sailing. Or staying up past ten for that matter. So I took four days off (I INTENDED to take four days off...) and help one of my pals deliver his and his wife's shiny new sailboat from Bay City to Petoskey.

I met these proud new boat owners through drinking, of all things. Susan and Rocky would come into a brewery that I used to bartend in a few years ago.

These two are the kind of people that instantly made my day better just by walking in the door.

The more they came in, the more I knew we would be friends for life. These two were some of the people I was most worried about losing after "the lie."

Thankfully that didn't happen. They are also the couple that I have to thank for getting me to "Damn Dirty Hippie Fest" aka Blissfest. (Yes, I hope to go back someday.)

Susan and Rocky are sailors that temporarily lost their way and slipped into the malaise known as power boating.

Please don't judge them harshly, I assure you that they are fantastic people.

We all have moments of weakness.

Last summer, Susan went for a sail on my friend's, Mike and Nancy's boat.

It was a perfect day and decisions were made. Not sure if their powerboat was for sale THAT day as it was a Sunday but it was definitely soon after.

The search was on. Boat shopping is almost as fun as boat buying which is almost as fun as boat selling.

Rocky went to work and found a beautiful boat last winter.

Buying a boat in the winter is like getting a bike for Christmas.

A cruel trick but worth it once spring arrives. After some discussion and a few hilarious "planning" dinners, June 16th was picked as the starting date of the maiden voyage.

Mike (of Mike and Nancy fame) and I drove down after work Thursday night for a gourmet dinner of McDonald's and an evening tour of thriving downtown Bay City. I don't THINK there are any bullet holes in Susan's Audi...

A quick 6am breakfast at the "Police Are On Their Way Inn and Suites" and down to the boat. She is beautiful. A breathtaking yacht.

Susan and Rocky are exchanging spousal pleasantries while Mike and I grin and go about our chores.
The only reason we are grinning is because we understand the pleasantries but are not currently plagued by them. We hustle up, get away from the dock and make the 7:15 bridge just as planned.
It was a beautiful morning and the three amigos were settling in for a few days of stories and sailing. We were off to a great start.

Rocky was happily driving his new boat all over the river while Mike and I rigged the sail.

Nothing quite like hoisting a crinkly new sail.

I imagine the sound of a brand new sail going up is something akin to the sound of angels singing…

It really seemed like things were falling into place exactly as they were supposed to.

The breeze was super light which gave us time to rig things and enjoy caffeinated beverages and some fun size Twix.

The boat just seemed to give each of us our own tasks. I nerded out on the radar and navigation systems while Mike rigged and Rocky sailed.

Zen type stuff for sailors.

The breeze built throughout the day and the sun burned through the remaining clouds.
Soon enough, the engine was killed and we were making 7 knots downwind on our way home.

It was perfect. Until it wasn't.

There was intermittent cell service up the shore of Lake Huron.

We are all weather freaks and none of us the hero type that would intentionally sail into a storm.

Bad weather wasn't predicted but as all Michiganders know, that doesn't mean much.

The breeze was about 11 knots out of the south and the autopilot sailed untouched for 4 or 5 hours at one stretch.

The skies continued to darken to the north and my Dad sent me a message that he was getting nasty weather including hail at his house about 45 miles to the west.

The wind started to clock to the north and the temp started to fall.

Mike called for a sail drop so I took her head to wind and down it came.

Everyone put their foulies on and in a rare stroke of good judgment, our life jackets and harnesses. Better safe than sorry, especially before you need it. Those words haven't always come out of my mouth.
The wind was now out of the north at 30 knots. Skies were getting progressively darker and weather radar showed some ugliness to the northwest.

None of us were concerned about the coming rain or wind.

Mike jinxed us (I'm totally blaming him) because he remarked that lightning was the only real concern he had. The skies were unlike anything I'd seen before.

Hues of yellow and blue that are beautiful but ominous. You could see the rain coming toward us.

Soon, shore disappeared behind a wall of water.

The sky would light up with lightning from time to time but no cloud to ground strikes.

The wind was up, it was raining and the lake was stirred up but still nothing terrifying.

I turned around in my seat, one hand on the wheel and one on my phone because I HAD to get a pic of the sky behind us, then it happened.

It is impossible to describe it accurately but I heard a sizzling hiss for about a millisecond before the loudest BOOM I've ever experienced exploded around us.

The GPS receiver exploded in a shower of sparks on the stern, the navigation screen exploded in front of me and for a moment, complete shell-shock hit.

We took a direct lightning strike. I could see Mike and Rocky talking but couldn't hear a damn thing they were saying.

Everybody was OK and through the chaos, something amazing happened: not one person panicked.

All electronics were fried but the diesel engine didn't miss a beat.

Just like earlier in the day, everyone got to work. Rocky started checking to see if we were taking on water, Mike grabbed the wheel and I started navigating us to a marina that was shrouded by torrential rains.

The winds were up to 40 and 50 knots but everyone was cool and doing their jobs.

I called the Harrisville marina and thankfully, the dedicated harbor master left his cell number on the answering machine.

Rocky dialed him up and my new friend "Ferg" was there to help us in.

I won't bore you with the rest of the story but once docked we could see some of the damage.

The top of the mast was a destroyed piece of blackened metal.

There was molten aluminum sprayed all over the interior of the boat from the lightning exiting the mast, leaving a million little pinholes.

There was a fist sized hole just aft of the bow where the bolt left the boat.

That boat took a full-on strike and kept it's sailors safe. She was sturdy enough that we motored her to Alpena, 40ish miles away, the next morning.

What does this lengthy tale have to do with addiction? Let's see if I can tie this all together...

That sail up the coast was perfect. Everything was going flawlessly. The wind direction couldn't have been more favorable.

The sun was gorgeous. I was sailing with two of my best pals. I even worked in TWO naps!

That combination of goodness is what recovery feels like when it's right.

That perfect wind direction is what we addicts experience once we finally surrender and stop fighting.

Moving through life with the wind at your back is so much easier than fighting the headwind we know as the insanity of active addiction.

We can get where we want to go but we also may have to make a few jibes and now understand that it's ok. We can't control everything so we adjust our sales and continue forward.

The warmth of the sun on your face is what we experience once we start to "thaw out"."

The amount of shame we carry combined with depression (for some of us) makes for a cold, dark place in our hearts, minds and souls.

The boat may look shiny and ship shape on the outside but inside she is a musty mess with serious structural issues.

Sometimes not fit to sail.

Sailing with such cherished friends is a luxury few are afforded. Addiction is an isolating disease. We crave the company of friends yet want to be alone at the same time. Solitude is a prison yet crowds are a living nightmare.

Once again, the insanity that is addiction.

Recovery allows us to just "be."

I was able to enjoy the boisterous tall tales in the cockpit as well as the quiet lapping of the waves on the bow as we sailed on. Two completely different but equally beautiful experiences.

That lightning strike was a poignant reminder of how fragile life truly is. Three guys could have ceased to exist had things gone just slightly differently.

There were no rookie sailors on board. Experience, trust, faith and blind ass luck got us through.

Sounds a little like the systems that a solid recovery program has built in. The ratios may be a little different but the ingredients are the same, trust me.

That building storm was very symbolic of what I presume a relapse is. Things kept getting worse. Conditions deteriorated. People were warning us. Then the lightning hit. Luckily we took "steps" to prepare for the worst. The lightning was a come to Jesus moment.

Our "steps" allowed us to sail another day. Recovery is very much like sailing in that it is amazing when it is amazing and treacherous when it treacherous. The common denominator between the two?

The amount of effort you put in directly correlates to the experience coming out.

Not drinking is a great start but the alcoholic mind requires constant effort. Sometimes it's tiring but not nearly as exhausting as the alternative. The title of this chapter is important.
Serenity is something that I had finally achieved after months and months of recovery, reading and writing. I looked at how many times I referenced it in writings or hash tags on photos. It was a lot.

My serenity was interrupted because I stopped working on "me". I forgot that everyone is fighting something and that they deserve some understanding and patience. I forgot that I am still a work in progress and that there is still much to do.

I forgot to look at the colors of the sunset while listening to the waves and smelling that Lake Michigan water. I forgot to put the effort in so I could enjoy the reward that is serenity. "Serenity" is also eerily the name of the boat in this story. She was perfect.

A dream of a boat. The damage to her is more extensive than we knew. In the end, the insurance company totaled her because the damage was too expensive to fix.

The three of us are very fortunate to be alive. Oddly that didn't fully hit me until a couple days later.

That boat sacrificed herself for us. Serenity is interrupted. Work must commence to see how best to let Serenity begin once more.

I need to take the time to say a huge thank you to my new friend, Ferg Ferguson of Harrisville Marina fame.

Ferg, you were a true savior in our time of need and I can't begin to thank you enough for your kindness and assistance.

The fact that you wanted a confirmation call once we arrived in Alpena safe and sound showed me even more what a stand up guy you are.

Look forward to meeting up again on more favorable terms, sir!

Stay sturdy!

27 I'M CURED!

07.23.17

Got some great news from an expert in alcoholism the other day. I'm cured!!!

Yep, I have put in enough time and work that I can now officially have a drink or two a week with no problem. Isn't that great news???

Not sure what to have first because it's been so long. Plus if I can only have a couple each week, I definitely don't want to waste my chances. It's been pretty warm lately so maybe I'll have a nice cold beer after work.

Wait, I know! It's time for some sailing so maybe a delicious rum drink. Not too strong of course because I have to be careful. No, wait! I was at dinner the other night and a guy at the table next to me ordered a scotch on the rocks.
One of my favorites! Heck, it was the same night I got my good news so that would make sense. I'll wait until Friday of course.

That way I won't become an alcoholic again. Perfect! It feels so good to be cured. It was a real battle. Today is 17 months sober. There are *Old Timers* at the clubhouse that have 30 and 40+ years of sobriety and still aren't cured. I can't imagine having to go on being sick that long. One of my buddies at work had his wife leave him.

Wanted me to have a beer with him. Now I can!

If I accidentally have three drinks this week, I'll only have one next week to make sure things stay balanced.

And definitely only on Friday or Saturday.

No school days!

There is also a wine tasting at a charity dinner I'm attending. It's on a Thursday but I'm sure they won't be pouring giant glasses of wine and since it's for charity and I don't want to be rude I'll just have zero drinks the following week. Wednesday night is race night! Almost forgot! I told the guys on the boat once I was cured, I would have a beer with them.

They are going to be so happy that I'm all better. One beer with the crew won't hurt.

I know it's Wednesday but is a special occasion so just this once, I'll bend the rules.

No drinks for two weeks after that because I can quit anytime I want.

Dang it. Tuesday we are doing a cookout for work.

Some of the guys don't know that I was sick. Don't want them to feel awkward or ruin the party.

I'll do a quick shot and a beer then be done for sure.

Oops. Forgot that my favorite restaurant is having my favorite special Monday night.

One that goes perfectly with a custom made margarita! This week is just an anomaly.

It's just the first week I've been cured so after this week passes, I'll just take it easy for a few weeks.

See??? It's all planned out so no problem.

Good thing I talked this out with you guys!

Without proper planning and discipline, I could get sick again and I don't think any of us want that.

Cured. Right... Wouldn't that be terrific?

See how insidious this condition is?
See how the alcoholic brain works against everything we work for? My brain is trying to trick me into thinking the very poison that almost killed me is actually much needed medicine. *It's exhausting.*

Funny how rarely I've thought about drinking these past 17 months. The *Old Timers* told me it would come and it did.

They seem to be right far more often than not. Thankfully they warned me. There are warning signs for relapse. My friend Scott started a small group that would meet after the Saturday morning men's meeting.

The "extra credit" meetings I've written about. He was also kind enough to spend some one on one time with me. Showed me a relapse prevention program.

Not sure I would have fallen off the wagon without it or not but I am so thankful that I didn't have to find out. Humans are not robots. We wear down and that's exactly what's happening. I'm tired.

Work is incredibly stressful. The annual summertime invasion of our little town is in full swing and the out-of-towers seem a bit more dick-ish than normal.

My one day off each week is Sunday and lately they have been partially off or nasty weather so no sailing. Right now it's easier to retaliate against a shitty person as opposed to trying to remember that they are fighting their own fight. That's not fair to them and it's a warning sign. My stupid brain is "adjusting" itself to the old way. "Don't worry, Derek. You are better now. That person continues to treat you shitty?

To hell with 'em. Let them have it. They deserve it." Not cured. Better but not the best.

I have to give in to win again. Get back to meetings. I need them right now and that's ok. It's not weak or shameful to go and it helps.

I'm going to write notes of gratitude and stick them on my fridge, computer screen, steering wheel and forehead. (for when I'm drying my hair) I'm going to reach out to people to say thank you. I'm going to reach out to people and apologize. I'm not going to drink.

Things are going better than they have in years and I'm whining. Warning sign if I ever saw one. So today, I'll start with my gratitude for you beautiful people. Thank you for the countless messages of support.

You help me make it through some incredibly challenging times.

My apologies for the complaining. Writing that stuff down helped me figure out what I need to do to get back on track. Kinda scary how fast we can go from “cured” to “sick” to on the mend, isn’t it?

Have a plan AND have your people in place and we can all succeed together.

28 ANALOG VS DIGITAL

08.29.17

By a show of hands, who out there believes that records sound better than CDs? Seems we have lots of people out there that do a great job of following directions! You can put your hands down now.

Please, you look a little silly...

I've heard the argument for and against each case. CDs are better because there is no imperfection from the needle and everyone knows how cool lasers are.

Albums are better because they are designed to recreate the music exactly as performed, imperfections and all. Here is my understanding of why people don't like digital reproductions: the digital "blocks" of data, regardless of how small, still can't reproduce the high and low peaks of original recordings.

My ears are not that finely tuned so the argument is wasted on me. The concept, is not. The concept is similar to what people in active addiction experience when we begin to thaw. It is a magically terrifying time in early recovery.

One of the reasons we use substances is to escape or numb reality. I think one thing we can all agree on is that reality has some pretty extreme highs and lows and being able to experience them in CD format is preferable at times. Reducing things to square blocks of data allows us to cope with the noise.

The trick with our "filter" aka our drug of choice, is that the small doses it takes to modify the live performance we know as life, increase as time goes by. The recording studio we record our lives in is full of delicious filters. Sometimes, regardless of the song, we lift the needle off the record, begging for peace and quiet.

Sometimes, tragically, the plug to our record player is ripped from the wall of life permanently.

I never realized how many "artists" this disease claims... But this is not a sad chapter!

Nope, it's one of observation and revelation! There are new, high tech devices that have been recently discovered in the last 70+ years to help us combine digital and analog into a symphony of living a great life. See how I used recently and 70+ years in the same context for some levity??? People are gifted and cursed with a variety of exaggerated senses.

This is something we share with you normals. I say exaggerated as opposed to heightened on purpose. Heightened makes it sounds like we have super powers.

(Yes, I know YOU have super powers but I'm trying to keep your secret identity safe!)

Some people have an ear for music. They can tell if the violin is a Stradivarius or a cheap knock off.

Thousands of dollars are spent on equipment to reproduce sounds that most of us wouldn't hear much less appreciate. "The reed in the tenor sax in second chair cracks about half way through this crescendo."

Probably an exaggeration but I couldn't tell there was more than one sax so... That level of sensory awareness, that reed-cracking pick up, is what starts to happen when we surrender and begin to thaw out. It's beautiful and painful at the same time.

Memories start seeping back in to the forefront of our consciousness. The memories are not just bad ones that we've forcefully suppressed; some are fantastic ones that we've suppressed. The record player starts playing...room quiet, volume up and the needle lands on the vinyl.
That hiss-pop sound crackles through the speakers as the needle catches the groove and away we go.

My son played T-ball when he was little and I helped coach the first year. Coaching T-ball at that age is mostly keeping the kids from digging holes in the outfield and chasing butterflies around the bases. It is incredibly cute.

The end of the season came and the other coach and I bought trophies for all of the players.

My kid was so proud of that trophy. The memory of him getting that trophy and jumping into my arms was so wonderful and so overwhelming.

As in tears in eyes overwhelming.

I had to pick the needle off the record on that one.

So intensely good but so much guilt for the things I missed out on. I got my act together and tried to put the needle back where I picked it up.

I wanted to finish the song but as with all broken down record players, the needle moved to a different part of the groove.

My daughter was three or four. Sitting on the floor in the living room coloring and singing.

Her mom grabbed me out of the office to listen.

The song went something like this, "Daddy, daddy, daddy, daddy...", on and on.

Happiest little girl in the world singing about her daddy. Two perfect "songs" ruined by their intensity.

How frustrating it is to finally get these memories back but have them be so vivid that they leave you in tears...

It's hard to explain how such happy thoughts can be so devastating.

Oh, I forgot to mention that they don't happen in the quiet solace of your home.

Not in the beginning.

They happen whenever that piece of your alcohol soaked brain repairs itself.

You don't get to pick.

I guess the closest I can get to an explanation for you normals is try to remember a time where you've been working tons of hours and are mentally and physically exhausted and you start drifting back to good and bad times.

Wishing you could replay the good tunes or rewrite the bad ones.
Now multiply that times 100. Here's the good news. CD technology is improving!
I can indulge in those super good memories in smaller, less intense data blocks of melodic goodness. If it gets to be too much, I can hit the pause button and pick up exactly where I left off later.

Now I have a "recovery equalizer" to help ease the highs and lows and fill in the mid range that alcohol used to occupy.

Every album comes with some yucky songs and that won't change but now that I'm converting my records to CDs, I have more control of the music library.

The bad songs are still in the library so they will still appear in the rotation from time to time.

I can experience a little of the yucky song or skip it all together and do each with a bit more precision.

It takes effort but now it can be done.

The *Old Timers* are incredibly accomplished audiophiles and are teaching me how to listen to the songs of my life instead of just hearing them.

The best part of long term recovery is now I get to write a soundtrack that I can be proud of.

29 IS YOUR FOUNDATION PREPARED?

11.11.17

Flying from Chicago to San Francisco. For a wine dinner. I used to love both. Sitting in the middle seat next to steroid - muscle flexing - fidget the whole time - scratch your disgusting skin - bad breath mouth breather guy makes me hate flying.

I still love dinner though! Been a lot more focused on the book and I'm back to making progress.

Real progress. Like, I'm taking the month of December off to finish writing so we can publish this book type progress. No self induced pressure at all.

The good part is, now that it's written here, I am accountable and have to get it done.
Or else! My time at the cement plant project in Charlevoix is winding down and I'll be starting a new project in January.

December is dedicated to finishing the book and the rest of November will be tightening up loose ends to make December possible.

It's kind of strange how the closer I get to the end of my part of this project, the more I realize I will miss parts of it and the people.

There are things I've learned on site that I never dreamed of. I definitely learned that I still have a ways to go with the whole recovery thing.

Enough stress and mental exhaustion allowed me to forget that each person is fighting a battle unknown. That each person experiences good days and bad.

That each person deserves kindness. It also allowed me to slide back into thinking I'm closer to being the center of the universe than just a tiny part of it.

The *Old Timers* say that the drinking is just a part of our condition and they are right.

It's keeping our head and heart in the right condition that requires the most work.

The thoughtful mind is the foundation that my recovery rests on and like all important structures, it requires maintenance. I was walking the site the other day and came across a familiar structure that caught my eye a different way.

The new perspective made me think of the pieces and parts that make a building are much like the pieces and parts that make up a happy, healthy person.

This structure houses enormous machinery with incredible temperature swings and vibrations.

It's tall and wide and catches every ounce of breeze coming off

Lake Michigan. The closer you get to the top of it, the more you can feel it actually move when the wind is up. The loads on each piece of structure have to be immense.

It is a fascinating piece of engineering. Each piece is designed to work together and even though there are fail-safes built in, none would function without a properly prepared foundation.

Kind of like each of us.

What caught my eye that day was a guy tightening the nuts between the steel structure and the concrete foundation.

The way he was tightening them is what caused me to think about each of our own personal foundations and that I was clearly in need of a tightening up. He had a giant wrench attached to a nut and was striking said wrench with a sledge hammer.
Each time he hit the wrench, there was a unique sound. It wasn't some obvious clank or bang but more of a pronounced "tink."

The only way I can describe it is an industrial version of the cliché tapping of the water glasses at weddings. Not sure if that translates.
So here is a guy, dressed in full Carhartt bibs and jacket, tightening these giant nuts onto their respective bolts.

What better to do than stop him and ask what he is doing?

He was cool about it. Mostly. He said because of the newness of the structure, the vibrations caused by the machinery, the expansion and contraction due to heat and the harmonics caused by the wind, that the nuts needed to be tightened regularly until the new building took a set and the siding was put on.

The sledge hammer and specialized wrench was the only way to accomplish it properly.

I have no idea how many hundred thousand pounds of steel are in this building but to see how important the small attachment points are made me think. What have I been doing to maintain my recovery foundation, much less continue to tighten it up?

The honest answer is, not enough. Lately I have been in "good enough" mode.

Haven't had a drink in almost 21 months but I have cut back on the things that made that beginning of a foundation possible.

One of my bigger flaws is that I tend to find a process or procedure that works really well and once found, I immediately try to find a different way.

It's a known flaw but a bastard of a flaw to fix.

Sledgehammer worthy. I've found my excuse generator has been re-fired. Lots of hours on-site coupled with wrapping up two external projects before December 1st, coupled with adding a self imposed deadline to complete a book, coupled with trying to make sure I make time for others, coupled with just not enough down time.

There is zero time for rest and even though I know it is short term now, it has been a long year.

Working on recovery tends to take a back seat to the "important" stuff when the important stuff pays the bills and keeps loved ones happy. In reality, the foundation of recovery is what allows me to function at a level to pay the bills and keep loved ones happy.

It seems that I usually need an experience or event to alert me to the fact that my foundation is in need of maintenance. Cracks form over time and they are expected and can be planned for but they must be addressed before they become structural.
The problem with neglected cracks is that "stuff" gets in them and can force them into bigger cracks. Some of the "stuff" is random. Events that pop up or situations that are out of your control. Gunk that can be blown out easily with a 10 minute walk outside.

No phone, no nothing, just taking your brain for a walk. Remind yourself of the good things you have going on, remind yourself of the good people in your life and the gunk is out of the crack.

Recognizing what upset you, assessing the actions you took to remedy the situation and making a plan for what to do if it happens again allows you to clean out the crack, put some sealant in it and move forward.

Sometimes the "stuff" that gets in the cracks is more aggressive. Sometimes it can dissolve the sealant that you used on repaired cracks.

This "stuff" gets down deep and tries it's damnedest to force the crack wider.

A quick sweep of a broom or blast of air from a nozzle isn't going to get this stuff out. You have to dig deep and use bigger tools.

The 10 minute walk is a good start but this repair might take dinner with a friend or a call to mom or maybe even a meeting to clear out and repair.
We are surrounded by people that are pulling for us to succeed. When they say to reach out if you need help, they mean it, so do it.

I don't think these cracks are unique to people in recovery. Ever get to a point where you are so frustrated or angry with someone or something then take a look back and wonder if it was that person, place or thing that was actually what was bothering you?

I have to do that all the time.

Maintenance.

Not long after I started getting sober, a friend of mine who is an expert in the field of addiction started having once a month extra credit meetings after Saturday meetings.

One of these meetings, he handed out a relapse prevention plan worksheet. I liken the plan to a set of maintenance blueprints.

If you study the prints, you can avoid serious damage to the foundation and actually start to build on that well maintained structure.

Having that set of blueprints and studying them helped me figure out that I have some work to do.

Sitting in the middle seat of that airplane next to the guy I described at the beginning of this chapter was a huge red flag. I wasn't in control and the guy had the audacity to do things that bugged the hell out of me. Who's problem was it?

This guy was just living life. I was creeping back to being the center of the universe.

It was time to clean out the cracks and get to building again. So I did. Did some reading while I was in Cali. Had a great dinner with a new friend.

Started reworking this chapter. Got in touch with some loved ones from my past.

Maintenance. My journey back to Michigan was just as chaotic as my journey out and it didn't have to be. I like schedules.

I like structure. I like control. I had zero influence over any of those things.

Confused planning made for a stressful ride to the airport. I made my flight back to Detroit from San Fran by seven minutes.

SEVEN!!! Smooth flight back to Detroit Metro only to find my connecting flight to Traverse City was delayed. By three hours.

THREE!!! Seriously???

"Why are they doing this to ME, the center of the universe???"

Remember, I just started to repair the cracks, they weren't fixed, just identified.

I grabbed a bite of grease at Chili's then headed to my gate. Found a seat at the end of a row away from all people and sat down to be pissed off and tired.

Solid plan to work on stuff, right? I sat there texting friends and fuming. I just wanted to go home and be surrounded by my stuff. My tunes, my snacks, my people and my bed.

Then something incredible happened. Someone invaded my area of disgust and forced me to have a great trip in three little hours.

There was a young lady sitting at the opposite end of my row, waiting out the long delay.

She is the type that forces you to do the embarrassingly obvious double take.

I'm not even sure what transpired or why but as the gate started to fill, she ended up sitting one seat away from me. I offered the seat between as the "stuff chair" so she didn't have to have her bags on the floor. And maybe as a reason to say hello.

We started to chit chat and she told me she was coming back from a girl's weekend in Nashville. My expertly honed sense of judging went to work immediately. Super cute girl, girl's weekend in Nashville, lucky little thing hasn't a care in the world.

I was as wrong as I've ever been.

As we got to know each other bit by bit, she forced me to become a better person.

It seems that my new acquaintance had a tragic story that she built her own foundation of triumph on. She told me a story that made me want to just scoop her up and save her but by the end of our visit, I learned that she didn't need saving at all. She explained that she was a war widow.

She's a single mom with two beautiful little girls, four and five years old.

Her girl's weekend was a getaway with other war widows. Like people sharing like stories of strength and hope. And sadness.

She also told me how she's spoken to groups in Austin about her journey.

She's taking her tragedy and using it to help others. She's a foundation repair person and I'm guessing a life saver to the people she speaks to.

A sobering thought hit me as we chatted. In the "old days," I would have been pissed off about the delay and found an airport bar to get hammered in. I wouldn't have started off with the intent to get hammered but it would have happened. Then drive home after getting to TC.

I would have never met this person and would have lost out big time. My new state of living allowed me the opportunity to meet one of the most incredible people.

Without knowing or trying, this airport girl that I got to share the stuff chair with made me better. Inspired to work on my foundation again and to build on it. She made me realize that the work is important but it can be fun, too.

Hopefully this rambling tale lets some of you pull back, read your blueprints and get back to the rewarding task of foundation preparation.

Imagine the things you can build! Thank you for getting me back on track, airport girl.

You are appreciated more than you know.

30 DISHSOAP FOR THE SOUL

10.15.18

My nearly empty bottle of dish soap. That is what inspired me to write again. How the hell my brain operates, I'll never know... It's been an amazing year so far in lots of different ways. Thanks to you good people, this book took off like crazy.

My publishing consultant told me that as a self published author writing a basic memoir about a topic most don't want to speak about, I should count on selling about twenty to thirty copies beyond my close friends and family. So I wanted fifty.

I talk about managing expectations but still struggle with it from time to time. Do as I say, not as I do? Thanks to some tremendous friends and family, great newspapers and TV reporters, and fantastic local bookstores we are over 1500 copies in circulation.

It is still surreal to think about writing a book about recovery and having that many people respond to it. So THANK YOU to EVERYONE that made this year successful beyond expectations!

Dish soap.

How does a nearly empty bottle of dish soap inspire me to write a chapter? I've been picking away at the next book and I'm struggling. It isn't incredibly fun to write the first two parts.

The ending is a blast but getting to that part is a struggle. I am at a particularly yucky part at the moment. I saw my nearly empty bottle of dish soap sitting on the edge of my sink and a bunch of stuff started coming back. I'm a clean freak. Not to the point of a disorder (at least not that particular one) but I want my stuff and my self to be clean. Hate having dirty hands.

Hate wearing dirty clothes. Hate having a dirty house.

I can remember being at the race shop working on the race cars and the guys would rag on me about wearing a white t-shirt and not getting any grease on it throughout the day.

I didn’t see any good reason to be dirty. Have I established my need for things being clean? I suspect that part of that need is control. In my mind, I should be able to control how messy or how dirty "things" get.

If something was dirty or messy, it was wrong. I could clean it or tidy it up and make it right. The control belonged to ME.

I knew what was right and could make things that way.

Dirty clothes? Laundry soap. Dirty windows? Crystal Rain Windex.
(LOVE the smell of that stuff!)

Dirty dishes? Dish soap.

Dirty soul? Alcohol.

Three out of four of those solutions worked.

I was running out of dish soap. I would be very careful with how much I used. I needed the dishes to be clean but I couldn't do that giant, fulfilling squeeze into the sink. Not that I would do that because that is something an out of control person would do... I remember watching the soap run down the inside of the bottle and trying to guess how much would be there after it all "settled."

It would cling to the side of the bottle and take FOREVER to get to the bottom. Mind you, a new bottle of that soap was less than five bucks. Unfortunately, that five bucks was also almost half a fifth of cheap vodka.
I needed that alcohol to cleanse my soul. I'll get dish soap tomorrow. Clean dishes only made me feel better when they were put away and out of sight. Alcohol made me feel better all the time.

Except when it didn't. It got to the point where I was obsessing about how long that soap would last. It was another contributor to my depression. Stop buying booze and buy what you need, idiot!

Those rational thoughts were absent at that point. I was clinging to what was left of my life just like that soap was clinging to the side of that bottle.

Both sliding to the bottom where we were destined to be.

One by gravity, one by self-propulsion.

So the soap and I both did our thing.

"Why didn't you just quit drinking???"

"Why didn't you just ask me for help???"

Easy questions with the same answer for both. Because I couldn't.

To quit drinking or ask for help would mean the same thing: admitting that I was no longer in control. The ultimate failure.

The amount of pain people in active addiction are feeling is incredible. I haven't met one yet that hasn't wished they weren't fighting it. It's humiliating. It's embarrassing. It's debilitating. Try to picture yourself asking these questions out loud to the appropriate person:

"Why don't you just stop eating so much?"

"Why don't you just get over him/her?"

"Why don't you stop being sad?"

"Why don't you just man up and stop letting the bully get to you?"

I can't picture any of my friends saying those things to someone.

If you are reading this, I'm betting that you can't either. BUT...

Every person on that list has their own "bottle of soap" that they are clinging to and are watching it dwindle.

The tighter we try and hold on to what is slipping away, the faster it squeezes through our fingers and down the drain.

It doesn't have to be that way anymore. It's ok to not be in total control of everything and it's ok to be flawed.

The perfect people are flawed, they just don't think we can see it. It is our responsibility to check in on people. There are people BEGGING for help in a million different ways. If they are your friend, check on them. Even if they are a pain in the ass, check on them.

I don't care how good a friend you are to the person or if you only knew them a little back in the day.

You may have made an impact on them back then and a quick, "How ya doin'?" might just be the refill they need.

Dish soap for the soul.

Give that bottle a giant squeeze.

31 AM I USING THE RIGHT LENS?

11.03.18

I am a gadget guy. Love toys. I bought a Canon T3i camera about 5 years ago and still barely know how to use it. My phone camera does JUST fine for what I need. My pics aren't "photos" they are just pics. I am going to learn how to use this thing someday though. Seems silly not to. I AM using it as inspiration currently. I had to move it to get to my drone (another toy I don't need but really like playing with) so I brought it out to charge it and of course, play with it. What I discovered is that the people that make their living with cameras like this definitely earn it.

There is a LOT of technology packed into this thing. The part that really grabbed my attention this time was the lens. I decided to look into it while cranking the thing back and forth.

There is a lot going on in there! So much that it gave me an idea for a new chapter... I have been struggling with the snapshots of humanity that my brain has been taking recently.

My life is VERY "people-y" right now. I know that isn't a word but

I can't seem to come up with a better one. Searching for a word allows me to indulge my procrastination gene so I made that one up. It means that I am not able to hole up in the Cottage of Solitude and isolate.

One of the things that has been most challenging for this recoveree is rotating back into society.

Quiet spaces are comfortable. Places with people of my choosing are comfortable.

The fact that I am not independently wealthy makes those two places the exception, not the rule. Back to the snapshots. In this book I talk about giving people the benefit of the doubt, giving them a little space, being gracious, etc.

All very good things and all very important things. Things I am REALLY struggling with right now.

This is a hard chapter to write because as a recovery coach, I'm allegedly supposed to have all the answers, apply them in my daily life and be genuinely happy all the time. Admitting that those things aren't happening feels like a failure.

The difference between the old me and Chow 2.0 is that I know it isn't a failure, just something that needs attention and adjustment.

Maybe some focus.

A lens change.

I see the brain as the camera itself. The part that interprets and processes the images that are seen through various lenses.

Some cameras are better than others. Some are in pristine

condition even though they aren't the newest model. Well maintained, high end gear may not have all the bells and whistles but it still performs at a very high level. The best gear with fastest processors and advanced functions won't perform as well if they have been dropped or mishandled or as in my case, wet.

Electronics respond to water much the same as a brain responds to alcohol. Fortunately, repairs can be made. The trick is remembering that post repair maintenance is just as important as the repair itself.

The camera can only interpret the images that the lens give it.

The challenge is to make sure we are using the proper lens for each application. I ask in advance for poetic license when it comes to lens names and functions.

The Telephoto Lens: this is the one that we use with our acquaintances and people we don't know well. We see them and how they act from far away.

We can bring them into closer view if we choose but this is a mid to long range lens.

Getting in too tight with this lens will make most of us feel awkward because we are probably seeing things that aren't meant for us to see.

Snapshots taken from far away can be made to look sensational but may not be accurate or in proper frame of focus. Most people use this lens appropriately because it gives us all we need.

It's the "How are you doing? I'm great!" lens. We don't need a lot of close up detail on that pic because we are satisfied with the data that is collected.

The photo looks good and we are on our way. The Zoom Lens: this is the one we use with our loved ones and those close to us.

We want the up close detail. I need to see if my kids are ok. I like to see my friends succeeding. It makes me happy to see the smile lines on my mom and dad's faces. I also need to see if any of the above conditions aren't being met. This lens will usually let a person see enough detail that problems can be discovered and hopefully dealt with before they get bigger.

The closer you are to your subject, the better this lens works. This is the "How are you doing and don't bullshit me." lens.

You want the close up detail on that pic because the subjects you are snapping are very important to you.

The Selfie Lens: quite possibly the most misunderstood and challenging lens to use.

It's a necessary lens but it has to be used with care. We need to take hypothetical snapshots of ourselves from time to time. It helps us measure our well being, physical and mental. A photo album of snapshots allows us to trend things.

Time lapse photography of your life. This lens is a good tool but like any other tool, needs to be used appropriately.

Now I realize that there are a million different lenses that do a million different things but these are the main bits in my kit. Here's how I am using them TOTALLY wrong at the moment and am reintroducing myself to them one by one. I'm using the telephoto lens on my friends and family. I am doing that because I am a bit overwhelmed with all of the peopling I'm doing at the moment and it's an easy cop out.

I can take a snapshot whether it be via social media (the worst darkroom ever) or a text.

It makes me feel like I'm still taking the photos even though they are being shot TOTALLY wrong and there are things I know I am missing.
It helps assuage the guilt though so it's good enough, right? I'm using the zoom lens on total strangers and acquaintances.
Using this lens incorrectly is incredibly damaging. For myself AND the subject.

This lens allows for some incredibly nasty judging of strangers and it isn't fair to them.

Trying to figure out why someone is acting like a jerk by focusing in tightly isn't helping either one of us. The very same person shot with a telephoto lens would be seen completely differently.

The zoom lens becomes a tool for judgment. More often than not, the jerk is holding the camera.

I'm not using the selfie lens at all at the moment. Because I'm fine. It's not me, it's them.

Which I know to be garbage.
Being a numbers guy, I can do some quick math to determine the probability of everyone else being off and me being on is zero.

But I HATE the selfie lens!

If I use it like it is designed to be used, it helps keep me on track. Take a daily snapshot. Holy shit, man. You don't look so good.

I can make adjustments if I keep current on stuff. That whole "time lapse of life" shot. Life keeps moving forward so keep taking the pics or else you lose the time and life just lapses. Yesterday I finally asked someone for help. I couldn't get the lenses right, the shots I was taking lacked focus and there were far too many of them. I have a written script for my "photo shoot" of life for the next few months.

Yep, I asked for help and am getting back to what works.

Small adjustments but wow things are coming into focus.

32 AN OPEN LETTER TO THE "OTHER SIDE"

02.07.19

One of the things we in recovery talk about a lot, and rightly so, is the impact of our action AND our inaction.

We talk about our guilt.
We talk about acceptance of our past.
We talk about the damage we've done and the people we've hurt.
We talk about all of this "stuff" with other people in recovery and counselors and coaches and clergy.
We do this talking to heal.
We do this talking to start rebuilding.
We do this talking so we can begin to move on.
We also try and talk to those we've hurt.
Sometimes we talk seeking forgiveness, sometimes just understanding.
Too often we talk but don't listen.
WE are ready to talk. Eager to talk.
So excited to be free from the chains of addiction that we can't stop talking.
Years of bottling up every feeling is over.
We've been given permission to let it out.

However... We fail in three very important areas when we decide to start our release:

1) We do the talking because WE are ready
2) We expect everyone on "the other side" to be ready to listen
3) We don't listen

My hope is that the letter that follows helps to remedy the three failures.

It is written for understanding, not apology.
It is written so those of you on the other side can "listen" when you are ready.
It is written so that you can listen to as much or as little as you want.
It is written so you can come back to the conversation if it gets to be too much.
I hope that it works like I want it to...
Dear everyone on "the other side", I hope you had a good day today. Lots of challenges on this end but none were insurmountable thanks to being in recovery.
The clear head and new ways of dealing with things are so very helpful.

If you are wondering what "the other side" is, it's those of you that aren't addicts, drunks, druggies, alcoholics or hopefully, those of us in long term recovery. It's been explained to me that being called "normals" or "normies" can be offensive and that is definitely not our intent.
We may still use those terms in the rooms but we say them with reverence and longing.

We love you and I mean that. The stuff you are about to "hear" is going to be uncomfortable.

It is going to be angering.
It is going to be saddening.
My hope is by the end of this letter, you will have a better understanding of our broken brains.
We don't want to be this way.
We don't want to be different.
Not like this. We don't want to have noisy brains.

The constant clatter in our heads is louder than gunfire. And it is there all the time.

We can see the look of wanting to help in your eyes, and it breaks our hearts as much or more than yours. We don't want to fail you.

You are the most important people in the world to us. It's not expectations you force on us, they are expectations we put on ourselves.
Our job is to succeed for you 100% of the time even though we know that is impossible. We don't want to have "one more" at the bar with acquaintances or "friends."

We want to come home to our loved ones. We know you want us to. We can't until we have "one more" because we blew it at work.

We wrecked the car.

We forgot to pick up the dry cleaning and now they are closed.

We lost the big contract or big client.
We got fired.

We know you want to see us but we can't understand why.

We don't like ourselves, why would someone as wonderful as you?

We don't want to sit in our vehicle at the end of our road, drinking or using and crying, waiting for you to turn the lights off in our kid's rooms and eventually ours.

We want to come home so bad but we can't because we are drunk or high.
We failed again and pray that you are asleep and won't notice our condition.

We brush our teeth with extra toothpaste and mouthwash and ease into bed so you won't wake up.

But you weren't sleeping. You were pretending to while tears rolled down your face.

We don't want to miss our children's games or programs or their anything. It never had anything to do with in laws or out laws being there.

It never had anything to do with having to work late.
It never had anything to do with wanting to drink or drug with our friends more than being at the event.

It had everything to do with us not being able to cope with crowds or noise or people that won't leave us alone so we can just talk to you and just watch our kids do their thing. We can't tell you these things because it would reveal how weak we were and that just can't happen.

Easier to numb the situation and get in an argument. If you get angry and chew us out, we can get angry back. That anger buries the fear of you finding out how weak we are.

We know we are wrong, we just can't back down and admit it. We don't want to ask for help. We know we can fix it if...

If we can just get that next client; if we can just get caught up on bills; if we can just get that promotion; if we can just make it through the next day without letting you down.

But we can't.

We can fix any other problem we face except ourselves. We wake up and see our biggest failure every single day. It's the first thing we see.

Today will be different. That is what we say. We want to believe it. But it isn't. And we know it won't be. We don't want you to leave.

You are the reason we exist. You are our strength and the reason we try at all.

We remember our early days and know if we just try harder, we can get that back. We try. And fail.

So to keep you from leaving, we push you away. Our broken brains decide that somehow it is better to force the people we love the most into the most awful position of leaving. We make you hate us.

We frustrate you and finally exhaust you until you have no other choice BUT to leave. We knew you would. Now we can put the shields up and not worry about being weak anymore.

We can't fail anyone anymore because we have finally succeeded in pushing you all away. Finally we have peace. Nothing to worry about anymore.

We don't want to be this way. But we are.

WE ARE THIS WAY. Those words are so hard to say and even harder to BELIEVE.

Those things you just read?

They don't have to happen anymore.

The pain we cause and the pain we feel doesn't have to happen anymore.

Recovery doesn't mean absolution, quite the opposite. There is a long road ahead.

The place the road leads is such a wonderful place. The destination makes the journey even more worth it. Long term recovery is where we are headed.

We know that some of you won't be coming with us because of what we have done in the past. That is pain we have to carry. We know that the pain we caused you doesn't magically evaporate because we are sober. We also know now that just because WE are ready to talk doesn't mean YOU are.

The difference is we are going to be here if and when you are. No more running. We are this way but we are working on it.

Progress, not perfection.

33 WE ARE THE OCEAN

07.04.19

"Enlightenment is when the wave realizes that it is the ocean." - Thich Nhat Hanh

I saw the above quote on one of my beautiful friend's social media account. I realize how fortunate I am to have seen it on her feed as it may not have made the same impact had it been somewhere else. Knowing the person helps know the message. Thank you for sharing this inspiration, M...

Haven't written anything of note in quite a long time. Life is being lived and things are good.

Stormy seas come and go but they don't throw me overboard anymore. It's not that the water doesn't get in the boat or that there isn't some seasick moments but no sail is perfect. We trim the sails to the breeze we have. That is how we navigate the sea of life.

The quote struck me. It was a different font, different background pic but the words struck me.

The quote struck me because I finally "got it." When the breeze is up and the waves rearrange the rocks on my beach, you can hear the water draining back into the lake. It is a unique sound and impossible for me to describe other than magical.

Now I know what that sound is.

The sound is the wave realizing that it IS the body of water it rides on. The wave is saying, "Shhhh...it's not over. My work isn't done.

I'm just rearranging my energy to apply other places."

I asked for thoughts from my social media family on what the quote meant to them.

"We are already whole. We just need to know it."
"Connection."
"We are all one."
"We are capable of more than we sometimes think."
"We are stronger than we believe."
These are all great interpretations.
I love how the same words mean so many different things to other people. It's a good reminder that we are all different and maybe, just maybe, different isn't wrong, it's just different.

We should celebrate that a bit more. Here's my take on what the quote meant.

It's different than the quotes from social media but I am celebrating their difference while sharing my own. Let's see if it works.
The wave IS the ocean.

It isn't a singular event that has a start and a finish. It is the start and the finish and the start again. The wave, because it is the ocean, has an infinite amount of effects on the world around it.

The wave starts in the dark abyss, rising up from the bottom. The rise is slow but with purpose.

As it rises, it gently nudges a fish, startling it from stillness, sending it on a journey it otherwise wouldn't have experienced.

That fish swims along it's new path. It feeds and grows bigger and continues toward it's unknown destiny. One day, as a mom and son are sitting on the shore, casting into the ocean, the boy feels a tug on his line.

His eyes light up as he looks up at mom.

"I think I have a bite!" Mom coaches him to be patient until he is sure the bite is certain then set the hook. The boy fights the fight and reels in his prize.

Beaming with pride, he looks toward mom and exclaims, "I did it! I caught my first fish! Thank you mom! I love you!"

The mom hugs her son close as tears stream down her face. This is a big day for both of them. And the wave moves on...

A recently widowed man sits on his deck, looking out at the ocean. He is rolling through memories of his life. He is remembering life before his loss.

The love he shared and the love he lost. He tries to erase the vision of his wife wasting away to alcoholism. He grabs a pen and paper and starts a love letter.

He knows full well it will never be read by the earthly eyes of the woman he loves but he knows she is watching him write. He completes the letter, seals it in a bottle and heaves it into the sea.

He begins his healing process.

A familiar wave grabs the bottle and carries it away. And the wave moves on... An ocean away a father and daughter are floating around in a tiny sailboat.

The breeze isn't cooperating, the sea is flat and the dad is starting to feel bad that his little girl isn't having the success he wants her to. She is getting nervous that she can't make the boat go for her dad.

No words are being spoken. In truth, they are both just happy to be together but the lack of words is eroding the happiness of the day.

Suddenly, out of nowhere, a swell appears and turns the boat. Her eyes light up as she grips the wheel a little tighter and starts to do what she has seen her dad do a million times.

The breeze picks up just enough to fill the sails with wind and two hearts with joy.

And the wave moves on... The wave has traveled the ocean and sees the shore.

It suddenly feels that its existence is about to end. It tries to hold back from crashing. It's efforts delay the inevitable. It rises up and crests as it begins it's inevitable crash into the beach.

The crash is spectacular. Sunlight sparkles in each beautiful water droplet. Suddenly, the wave realizes that it's journey isn't over.

It whispers, "Shhhh...." as it retreats back into itself. As it does, it rearranges the rocks on the beach and exposes a beautiful, heart shaped stone.

A young man is walking along the beach and spots the stone, picks it up and puts it in his pocket. To him, it's a sign that he should go forward with his plan to ask his girl to marry him. And the wave moves on...

The wave is in the middle of an epiphany. It saw what it thought was the end yet it still existed. The energy it started with at the bottom of the ocean was still there. Retreating from the beach it crashed into was not a retreat at all but a regrouping.

Transmitting and receiving energy from its greater body. The wave begins its journey anew.
How does this relate to long term recovery?

When we start our journey to long term recovery, we often find that we are starting from a dark place.
A bottom. As we start to rise, we gather energy.
And we start to transfer that energy along the way.

We touch lives and don't even realize it. That energy is not finite and doesn't reduce in strength as it moves from point to point.

We don't have to directly touch people to affect them. Our recovery is a source of success and triumph for people directly and indirectly in our path.

The mom and her son were fishing because she saw someone she looked up to enter treatment and get their life back. The wave transmitted the power of courage.

The widower was able to start his healing process because a book he read said it was ok and that it wasn't his fault.

The wave transmitted the power of grace. The father was able to sail with his daughter because he saw the happy people pouring out of a local twelve step meeting and he joined them.

The wave transmitted the power of acceptance. The young man was able to find the courage to ask his sweetheart to marry him because he was finally able to put his years of addiction and self loathing behind him. He realized that he was worthy.

The wave transmitted the power of forgiveness. The ocean is no different than the recovery community. There is an infinite amount of energy in both. Some good, some bad.

The great part is that the bulk of the energy is good. There are tsunamis that do tremendous amounts of damage just like there are people that do the same. They are the exception, not the rule.

The rebuild after the damage or destruction is always amazing and stronger than what was originally destroyed. There is a wave of awareness and acceptance building in our country right now.

We are starting to understand and ACCEPT that addiction is something that needs to be addressed and treated. And it needs to be addressed with kindness and positive energy. We have a long way to go but we are closer than we have ever been.

A woman is in the depths of despair. Her husband and kids left her months ago. Today she lost her job and the rent is due tomorrow.

She has struggled with addiction her whole life. Today she is tired. Exhausted psychologically, physically and spiritually. Today she is walking out into the ocean and not coming back.

She takes a few steps into the cold water and sees something glinting in the setting suns' last few rays. It's a bottle with something in it. A love letter.

Today that love is for her. Today she turns around and walks back to the shore. Today is the first day of the rest of her life. And the wave moves on...

34 WE ALL HAVE ROCKS

09.07.19

They say the nothing bad happens to a writer, it's all just material. Not sure about the veracity of that statement but for this chapter, it seems to fit. The other day the lake was rocking.

A big breeze blew all night and the waves were spectacular. Unfortunately, some spectacular waves and high lake levels wrecked the steps and platform that leads to my beach so I had to go to Plan B.

Plan B involved getting dressed for possible public interaction and driving a couple blocks to a different access. Plan B worked out just fine because instead of just tossing on enough clothes and some ratty sneakers, I considered some variables.

Mainly, getting wet during my adventure. Flip flops and bathing suit time. Hindsight has taught me that all future Plan Bs should also include a towel...

Parked the car, grabbed my camera (which oddly enough doubles as a cellular telephone, too) and headed for the stairs.

One of my friends has been struggling with a divorce and he recently posted something concerning on the Book of Faces.

I don't feel like giving them any additional free publicity so that is my clever name. I am an extraordinarily coordinated human being so walking down the steps to the lake is the perfect time to scroll the Book and look for his post to make sure I know what I am talking about before I message him to check in.

In reality, I am NOT an extraordinarily coordinated human so this was a horrible idea. I could either concentrate on walking (gum free) or scrolling.

I'm sure many of you that are familiar with the social media platform I speak of are also familiar with their convenient "People You May Know" feature. That feature popped up and distracted me from my search and from walking. So I stopped. I always like seeing who FB thinks I may know.
It is kind of funny when I see an overly attractive woman and see we have one friend in common. Yep, fake profile with a creepy friend. Come on, creepy friend! You are better than that!

So instead of cheering on Creepy Friend, I became him. Pretty girl crosses the screen. Nope, don't know her. Use the fat finger technique to scroll past and oh no… "request sent".
Yep, I became the creepy friend guy.

NEVER scroll and walk.

It is a hazardous pastime that doesn't always turn out well. But this time it did. My less than dexterous jabbing at my camera (yes, it also functions as a telephone) sent my brain into a panic.

Nothing I could do about it now. Time to head to the lake and watch the waves come crashing in. Luckily I forget about things pretty quickly so the errant request will probably disappear before I finish falling down the stairs. The lake is amazing.

The waves are not tidal waves but they are respectable four to six footers. The power in them is undeniable. Last year at this time I could walk out and around a little point on the beach but the water is high enough and the waves are big enough that I don't want to get bashed into the rocky shore.

Not adventuring around the point is part wisdom and part chicken.

Things don't heal as fast as they did when I was in my twenties.

And phones cost a thousand dollars instead of twenty bucks. I wander down what used to be beach but is now just roiling water.

The water can't get out as fast as the waves bring it in. It's fascinating to watch.

It can also be a little disorienting. Water swirls at your feet as waves bash into your side.

Maybe more chicken than wisdom at this point. I snap a bunch of pictures. The wind was blowing the tops of the waves as they crashed into the rocky cliff. The sun was up just enough to where it wasn't hitting the lake but it WAS hitting the froth created by the cresting wave and the blowing wind.

The sparkle that was happening was better than Fourth of July fireworks. I stayed down there until I got cold and tired from fighting the lake.

The lake will always win.

A nice warm car waited at the top of the steps. No messing with my phone at this point.
Get up the steps, get in the car and head home for a hot shower and a cup of coffee.
In that order because the beach was full of grit and sand.

I don't like having grit and sand on me.

Shower grabbed although I semi-regret washing some of the bigger bits of sand and rocks down the drain. I justified it as polishing grit for the plumbing.

Coffee in hand and I am ready to check out my pics from the lake adventure. Not sure why it took me so long to figure out that if I hold the button down on my camera, it takes pics until you let up.

It makes getting the right shot easier if you don't mind scrolling through hundreds of pics. The little notification light is blinking on my phone. I have a new text, a new FB message and a new FB alert. Text is about sailing stuff so that is excellent news.

The FB message is from a friend that needs an extra copy of this book for a friend of hers. Got it. The FB alert is a friend request from a pretty girl.
I don't know this person.

Oh no...it's the girl that I accidentally friend requested! She accepted! Now I feel even worse than if she had just declined. Social media is as wonderful as it is poisonous. I sent an apology message explaining my clumsiness.

The waves, the steps the fat finger, etc. She was very gracious and kind.
She saw that we had multiple friends in common and her words she figured, "why not"? Huh. Why not, indeed.. This whole thing

has thrown me way off.

I had a very specific plan and this was not part of my plan. Shower, coffee then edit pictures. Now I am clumsily visiting with a very kind stranger. I honestly don't think she could have been any more polite or understanding.

I sent her the picture of the wave before I shared it with my friends on FB and she remarked about how beautiful it was. I mentioned how kind of smart I was for preparing for my adventure by wearing the appropriate attire for getting wet but then how kind of dumb I was because the waves that were tossing the small rocks around REALLY didn't care that I was wearing flip flops instead of shoes.

Yep. Incredibly painful but I got the shot!

In my feeble attempt to be clever I said something dumb like, "It's nice to meet you and I hope you aren't a beautiful wave full of rocks."

Yep.

Typed it out and intentionally hit the send button. And that is where this chapter begins. Lots of back story but it really is important.

Her response? "Oh we all have rocks." Huh. Again. And with one statement, one prophetic, incredibly kind statement, she opened the dam that has been holding back this chapter.

The SECOND I read those five words I knew what she meant and what this chapter was going to be. "Oh we all have rocks." We do "all have rocks."

It's where we carry them that makes a huge difference. Some of us carry our rocks in our heads. We cannot accept that things can change if we are willing.

If we WANT them to. These rocks are damaging because the entire time we think we are protecting ourselves with our mighty rock wall, we are blocking helpful new ways of thinking. We are ALL fighting something.

We are ALL recovering from something. More often than not, there are different ways to fix something.

New ideas and new methods might just be the way to go. Maybe we just move one or two rocks at first.

Keep some familiar security and let the light of new concepts peek in. Some of us carry our rocks in our words. We use our words to hurt others to keep ourselves from being hurt. Hurting people hurt people.

We say hurtful things. We tell lies. We use awful words and phrases. We do this to keep people away.

We do this because we don't take the time to consider why someone may be acting a certain way that we don't like.

We do this to dismiss others so that we can get on with our lives because we are so busy. We do this to feel superior to others because we feel so awful about ourselves. If we are willing to ease up on our forward force fields, ease up on the hurtful words, some of the kind words that others have for us can get in.

Maybe there will BE more kind words for us if we stop going on offense all the time.

We are going to talk about words in the next chapter. Some of us carry our rocks in our hearts.

We have been hurt and are not about to feel that again. Not ever. We wall up our feelings so that nothing can get to them again. It is better to feel nothing than to feel pain. Feelings are weakness.

The bigger the rocks we use to build the wall around our hearts, the less chance someone can move them and get back in to hurt us again. Those rocks are cold. Humans weren't designed to be isolated creatures.

Can't we learn from the pain we have endured?

Can't we look at that hurt and see what our part was? Maybe if we see our part, learn from it and apply our lessons, we won't get hurt again. And maybe we won't hurt others. Some of us carry our rocks in our souls.

Only instead of a solid wall of stone, the rock crusher turns slowly, constantly smashing our already battered spirits. Boulders of guilt, denial, self loathing and worthlessness bash into our very core.

For some, the bashing will go on until our last breath. Sometimes that last breath comes sooner than it should. The combination of rocks in our heads, words and hearts will not allow our souls to let the healing light of day in. Especially when we need it most.

Do not despair. We really can start to set our rocks down. Not all of them and certainly not all at once. We CAN accept new ideas. We don't have to accept them all and certainly not all at once.

The old "I tried that and it doesn't work" can still be the attitude IF we are willing to try something else. YOU are in charge of you.

That also means YOU are responsible to take action. Start

choosing which rocks to take out of your head. We CAN change the words we use.

This is really important but really easy. It is so important that the entire next chapter is about word choice and phrasing. We can ease up on our full frontal assault. Maybe if we ease up on our hard words, the soft words others want to say to us can actually be said. And heard. No matter how bleak our situations or how awful and irrecoverable we may feel, there are people that like us. Change your words and change your life.

We CAN start to feel again. Slow and steady wins this race. Protecting ourselves is important. So is letting other people. Good people want people to succeed. Good people instinctively want to help others. Once we start to take the rocks out of our heads and out of our words, the heart is a natural third step. New ways of doing things are succeeding. New words are attracting new people.

New feelings are possible. When we are ready.

We CAN start to like ourselves again.

We can stop adding rocks to the crusher and turn it off once and for all. We can engage in self care and begin to forgive ourselves. It is easier to forgive others but equally important to forgive ourselves.

We are worthy and it is ok to like ourselves again.

New ideas, new words and new feelings are now part of the foundation of our shiny new souls. Is this the only way to get where we want to be? Nah.

It's one of many. Are there still going to be people that sneak rocks into our back pockets as we unload the ones we already have? Yep. But now it's ok to turn around and say, "Enough."

We should probably try and use our new, nicer words when speaking to them though. The message here is that yes, we all have rocks and they are heavy.

Maybe they have served their purpose and it is time to start setting them down. If not for the kindness and wisdom of a person I've never met, I don't think this chapter could have happened.

Thank you for not throwing rocks, kind stranger.

35 LET'S TALK ABOUT HOW WE TALK ABOUT IT

09.17.19

I have to admit something. I used to use all the wrong words. Sometimes they still slip out. Sometimes a few cuss words even slip out. I'm not working as diligently on that condition.

I've taken enough psychology and marketing classes and been to enough sales seminars that I know word choice matters.

There is scientific evidence that it does and it proves out in sales success. Never considered how important it could be in the world of recovery. Not once. Not until I took my first class on my way to becoming a Recovery Coach Professional.

Every class in the series touches on word choice. Every one. Some more than others but they all talk about it. So after an extended time of using the new words and ideas, I really feel like they are taking hold AND I'm finding out that they do matter.

Not just to the person suffering from substance use disorder but to the people around them AND society as a whole. Word choice is important in removing stigma. Eyes are opening about the crisis we are facing when it comes to substance use disorder. People are starting to see that others need help.

Stigma hinders understanding. Hopefully this chapter will help demonstrate how words can be helpful. The words we are going to discuss aren't "industry standard" changes and some may seem a bit trivial but I think overall, they help us take positives steps toward helping each other navigate this challenging world of addiction. Let's start with the big one: addict.

That word carries so many negative connotations. To me, addict is a label that describes hopelessness. "If I am addicted to something, that means I can't live without it and there is no hope of changing how I live my life so I might as well give up."

I can't imagine my parents telling people that I am an addict. I CAN imagine them telling people that I am in recovery from substance use disorder. I can imagine them telling people that I was addicted to alcohol but through numerous different methods, I am living a healthy life in long term recovery.

I can imagine them telling people they are proud of me again. "If I have substance use disorder, there are methods and treatments available for my condition so there is LOTS of hope of changing how I live my life and I will NOT give up."

For way too long, the term "addiction" and its derivatives have carried stigmatizing, negative connotations. It's understandable. Substance use disorder can be an ugly, uncomfortable thing to talk about.

Remember way back at the beginning of the book when I talked about how hard it was to walk into an AA meeting for the first time for the second time?

Too often our words and attitudes keep people from walking through the door of whatever treatment might save their lives. Seeking treatment for a life threatening disease should be reason for celebration and hope, not shame and disgust.

"Look at Joe getting help for his condition. Good for him!!! I hope he pulls through!!!" We say it for people with cancer, we can say it for our friends and family with substance use disorder.
How about this word to describe someone: clean.

"Did you see that Jane got clean?"

Are you saying that Jane was dirty before? Jane may have been physically dirty because of where her disease took her but that is the extent of it. Jane is and always was a human being. She is someone's little girl no matter her age. She is someone's sister.

She is someone's mom.

Her heart and soul were NEVER dirty. Jane was numbing pain that we don't know about. She has substance use disorder but she didn't "get clean." She worked her ass off to find life in recovery.

How much better does she feel when she gets to talk about recovery as opposed to talking about "being clean...?" How much more hope does she have in her heart when she knows that recovery is right there waiting if she has a reoccurrence of use?

She wasn't dirty, she needed extra help. Jane is a human being that wants to live in long term recovery and it is our job to help her. Here's one I really dislike: relapse. "Joe was in recovery for almost five years but he relapsed." AND? Why did he have a reoccurrence? What changed in his life? Joe had a reoccurrence of use, not a relapse. "Relapse" is a word that goes hand in hand with "failure."

Joe didn't fail. Joe had a reoccurrence of use.
Reoccurrence if you want to shorten it up. Yes it takes longer to say. It isn't as easy to blurt out quickly when trying to point out how sad a case Joe is.

Which one sounds better? "Did you hear that ole' Joe had a relapse after damn near five years of being sober? I knew he couldn't stick with it forever."

Or... "Did you hear that Joe had a reoccurrence? He's been in recovery for almost five years and doing really well. I wonder what changed in his life?"

Joe relapsed because we just knew he couldn't make it. We predicted it and guess what?

We were right. This terminates our responsibility to help Joe and we move on with our lives.

Joe had a reoccurrence so something changed.

We recognize that Joe has been doing well but something must have changed. Something changed because we have faith in Joe and we know he wouldn't have a reoccurrence just for fun.

This gives us the ability to at minimum, start a conversation on how best to help Joe.

Personally, if I hear that a friend has had a reoccurrence of use, I am going to reach out. I don't care if it's true or not. Probably going to sound something like this...
"Joe, it's Chow. I heard that you might be having a hard time with

your recovery. Not sure if it's true or not. Honestly don't care.

All I care about is how you are doing. What's going on in your life?" Is that how we speak in normal conversation? Probably not.

Can we get there with practice? Probably so. These are just some of the bigger ones we can adjust to.

It's a start. For too long, substance use disorder has been a shame-based illness SMOTHERED in stigma.

Stigma isolates individuals and their families because people start to believe the words others use to describe them. It encourages people to deny a fatal illness and ignore symptoms because we don't want to be that label. Stigma comes from every angle imaginable.

It comes from outside the recovery community. It comes from treatment providers and programs. It even comes from within the recovery community itself! Wanna take a guess at the most damaging place stigma comes from? It comes from within ourselves.

I can talk myself out of going out for ice cream if I let the brain spin up too much. There will be a lot of traffic. There will be a lot of people that I know there.

I am a little chunky and don't really deserve an ice cream. I don't want people seeing me eating ice cream.
I'll go out for ice cream tomorrow. I LOVE ice cream and can talk myself out of going for one!

Now imagine if I replaced ice cream with treatment.

There will be a lot of traffic. There will be a lot of people that I know there. I have lost everything because of my condition and I don't really deserve treatment.

I don't want people to see me seeking treatment.

I'll start treatment tomorrow.

People we call "alcoholics", "drunks", "druggies", "junkies" and "addicts" tend to hide because of stigma and shame.
People we recognize as humans with substance use disorder tend to be more responsive to assistance because we see them as humans.

Word choice is a subtle but powerful tool in our bag of tricks to help each other.

Choose your words.

36 MATH IS HARD

09.24.19

The words above will have changed a million times before they actually became the title. The two previous chapters built to this one. New ways of thinking and feeling. New words to describe the world and people around us.

Now we are going to see how all that new stuff intertwines with people in recovery (from whatever malady we suffer from) and the people in our lives.

The journey we are taking together makes both sides of the equation very nervous. We are changing preconceived notions and commonly accepted societal norms. Both sides are surrendering.

We aren't surrendering hope or love or accountability. We are surrendering control. That is probably challenging to read and more challenging to accept. I get it. Let's keep going and hopefully by the end of this chapter, you will all be more comfortable with this concept. There are lots of experts out there.

Experts in every field. Experts lined up to tell you how to do things. How to make millions.

How to be prettier.
How to be skinnier.
How to be stronger.
How to be smarter.
How to get sober.
How to do it the right way.

The experts tell you what you are doing wrong and what to do to fix "it."

I may be the only one out there that feels this way but... I don't like being told what I'm doing wrong. I don't like being told what to do PERIOD.

"Derek, walk across this road right now and pick up that $100 bill. Do that and it is yours. No other obligations." Umm...no.

Would that free hundred bucks improve my life? Of course. Is it logical to immediately dismiss the idea of walking over there to pick up that money just because someone told me to?

Not at all.
Does anybody else remember/frequently use the saying, "You're not the boss of me!." from when we were kids???

How many of you have heard, "Why don't you just quit using *(insert drug of choice)?*"

How many of you have said that line to someone you love? How many of you have begged...

Doesn't it just make sense? If something is hurting you, you should just stop it.

If the stove is hot, it doesn't take you years to figure out to take your hand off of it. It doesn't take the loss of careers and family and homes to know that the stove is hot and it will burn you. Why can't we stop?

Why can't we use "common sense"? The sixty-four-thousand-dollar question.

First of all, I don't think there is any such thing as "common sense". If there was, we would all have it and it truly would be common.

I've seen some masters degree holders that couldn't pour piss out of a boot if the instructions were on the heel.

That's a Dad saying. Second of all, we can stop. We. Can. Stop. Recovery happens.

Some of us are going to go away to treatment for a period of time. We aren't calling it "rehab" anymore.
We are treating a very serious condition with hopes of gaining the tools to live life in long term recovery. Treatment times vary from person to person.

It doesn't matter.

The longer the treatment does NOT mean the shittier the human. Mom-Dad-Sister-Brother-Daughter-Son-Friend will be home before you know it no matter how long the recommended stay is.

Not everyone requires in-patient treatment. And that is ok. Some of us are going to start going to a 12 step meeting. Personally, I can say that AA saved my life. It was the perfect place for me to go and be safe from the chaos surrounding me. It gave me an hour of peace at a time.

It helped me figure out why I was doing what I was doing. It also provided that ray of sunshine that started to thaw my brain.

In the beginning, I went two to three times a day. Now I like to go to the speaker meetings once a month to see everyone and listen to the stories. AA is free and the coffee is plentiful.

The camaraderie is priceless. AA isn't for everyone. And that is ok. Some of us are going to start going to a counselor or therapist. We may be in groups or we may be one on one. Addiction is often tied to trauma.

Digging that trauma out and shining the light on it may be what is required for multiple reasons.

Heal that wound or wounds and begin to address the addiction. The confidentiality of one on one sharing can be very important to people. Sharing in a moderated group is a way to surrender some control and still retain the feeling of security. Counseling and therapy aren't for everyone.

And that's ok. Some of us are going to start meditating and doing yoga. We might need that silent introspective time.

Mind, body, spirit. Combining meditation, yoga and reading can be very effective for certain people. There is usually little to no sharing so it gets rid of some self induced pressure.

Meditating and yoga aren't for everyone. And that's ok. Some of us may enlist the help of a recovery coach. We might want the one on one approach.

We have surrendered control but we still like to be on equal footing with the person we are talking to.

We like the flexibility of trying different pathways to recovery. We like talking to someone with some shared experiences and that can gently, actively relate.

We like talking to the supportive, cheerleader type. Working with a recovery coach isn't for everyone. And that's ok. There are numerous pathways to recovery available and more come online all the time.

We are FINALLY starting to acknowledge that there is no one way that works for every single person. We may share a similar condition but that doesn't mean that we all respond the same way to methods of recovery. Now for those of you "dealing" with us...

There are resources for you as well. You are probably entering foreign territory.

You are not alone. Trying to understand us is almost impossible at first. Our behavior is irrational.

It's maddening. It's destructive. And you still want to help. Almost forty percent of my client base is "normal" people that are in some sort of relationship with a person in active addiction.

The questions they ask are heartbreakingly similar. Concerned parents, concerned spouses, concerned relatives. The common thread is substance use disorder but it is also exhaustion, fear, hopelessness and sometimes, surrender. And not the good kind.

All of the treatment methods that I listed above? They have a counterpart for you as well.

We are recognizing that people that love and support us need love and support as well.

The next couple pages are dedicated to those of you that choose to stay by our sides.

You are such a critical piece to this puzzle but we don't pay enough attention to you. I'm sorry that it is this way but I am going to really focus on changing that. You deserve it. Some of us are going to take longer than others. Some of us are going to need more help than others.
Some of us are afraid to admit our weakness to you. Some of us will want you to help us. Some of us won't. That last statement needs some of its own time. Some of us will want your help.

We will want to tell you about our meetings and what we talked about while we were there. We will want to start talking about feelings.

We will want to start making amends. We will want you to tell us how you feel but only a little bit at first. We will want you to be proud but not so proud like we are little kids just learning to ride a bike.

We will just want you to love us. Some of us won't want your help. And we are sorry that we don't. We can see it in your face that you want to.

And we love you even more for that but... We are embarrassed. We are embarrassed for YOU.

We have let lots of people down. We have let YOU down. We are starting to take ownership of our actions and it is very painful. We used to be proud and now we aren't. We will want to hide our treatment from you a little until we really start to believe it will help.

We have been conditioned to think that we should be punished for our actions but this new way is welcoming and supportive and completely foreign.

This is a process and it will take some time. We love you for being with us on the journey. We don't know what we want or how to get there just yet. We are chasing a moving target that we really can't see. We know you are frustrated.

We are frustrated, too. WITH ourselves and FOR you. There are going to be some incredibly hard parts for both of us in this process.

There will be times where we will want to give up and go back to the numbing. Some of us will give up and go back. That doesn't mean we want that more than you. It means we need to try again.

Maybe a different way. As we spend more and more time in recovery, we are going to get praise from more and more people. And you may not. And it isn't fair. We know that and are embarrassed.

We know your efforts. We know your suffering. It isn't fair but we are working on it.

We want people to know how important you are to our recovery. We are telling people how thankful we are for you, I promise.

This is a big chapter. Lots of "stuff". The reason is understanding for both sides of the equation. The equation that sounds like new math is really just simple addition. You + us + proper care for each = recovery for ALL Now like any math problem, there are variables. And the variables are variable.

See?

Math really IS hard.

You = mom, dad, sister, brother, spouse, significant other, friend

Us = people suffering from substance use disorder

Proper care for each = could be any one or combination of the things we talked about above

If you look at that equation, it shows it clearly. Everyone is on the same side of the equation, adding their part. The answer to the equation includes ALL of us.

Will things change between the variables? Probably. There is a lot of growth happening.

Does it have to be a negative thing?

Not at all.

One of the reasons for reworking this book is the knowledge I have gained in the time since it was published.

There are no more absolutes. Is abstinence the only way to recover? It is for me but that doesn't make it so for you. If therapy fails does that mean it always will? Nope.

If AA doesn't work for you, does that mean there is nothing else to try?

Nope. In the same breath, if AA doesn't work the first time (it didn't for me), does that mean you can't go back and give it another whirl?

Nope. Are we going to grow and change through whatever process we find that works?

YES. Are we allowed to change the pathway we utilize to continue that growth and change?

YES. Are all the variables in the equation allowed to change direction before failure happens?

YES. Can we seek recovery and have it stick before we hit the bottom?

YES. Finally, are human lives more important than conformity?

YES. My recovery coaching career has taught me that we can change methods and procedures and thought processes to fit each equation.

This is not a zero sum game.
If one method fails, that DOES NOT mean you did. We are all on a fantastic journey TOGETHER.

There IS hope.

We DO recover. ...

37 LIFE IS NOT A TASK LIST

September 2022

I heard this at coffee the other morning, "Life is not a list of tasks to be completed. Life is a beautiful project to lean into. It deserves your effort."

The gentleman that said it was emphatic about his statement and it resonated with me.

We aren't here to get everything done then expire. Life is something we need to experience, not endure. We start off giving our all, why not continue that?

We need mobility. We learn to crawl, then walk and then run. All three are key pieces to the project. None were easy. We were frustrated right from the beginning but did not give up.

We need communication. We need to be able to tell people what we are feeling, what we want and what we need.

We need connection. With our parents, our siblings, and our friends. That feeling of belonging. Loving and being loved.

We put all our effort into those things in the very beginning. All of it. What happened when we did that? We succeeded.

Next we started building those skills. Combining them. Mobility combined with communication expanded connection. That expanded connection improved our level of communication and as a result, our mobility.

The *"Triumvirate of Needs"* drives our decisions and behavior from beginning to end.

We can't wait to start school. Kindergarten will be so much fun! See our little friends every day. Playing and learning that was disguised as playing.

Our teachers reading to us.

Quiet/nap time and the best part of the day: snack! By the end of that year though we want more. The big kids get to go outside for recess. Big like six years old instead of five but still. They get to do more, and we want that. Kindergarten graduation achieved. Recess time, here we come!

Check that off the list...

Elementary school! New friends. Lunch in the cafeteria. A new lunchbox and everything! No more kindergarten babies. And we get to go outside and play!!! But...no more snack...no more nap... learning is no longer disguised as playing, it's actually work disguised as learning! What happened to the nice lady that told us EVERYTHING we did was great?!?!

What is this nonsense about staying in from recess because we were spending too much time "visiting with our neighbor"? We can't wait to get to junior high. Different teachers every hour. New "neighbors" to visit with. We will practically be grown-ups. New neighbors, here we come!

Check elementary school off the list.

Junior high, we have arrived! New friends to make. New routines. A locker! No more lunchbox though. Those are for little kids. Hot lunch for these cool kids. New subjects, class changes, all good stuff. Hey wait a second...we have to get up WAY earlier?

No Recess?

Our friends aren't in all our classes with us. HOMEWORK!?!?! No big deal.

This is a good step. Dances are a pretty good trade for recess. Standing awkwardly on opposite sides of the gym is way more fun than everyone playing kickball together. Kickball is a pursuit of children.

We are approaching adulthood and can't trifle with such things. Soon we will be in high school THEN we will be in charge.

Check junior high off the list.

High School! Finally!

Won't be long now and nobody will be telling us what to do. Our first jobs give us some walking around money. The holy grail of freedom is realized...the almighty driver's license!

Talk about mobility, communication and connection. The world suddenly got smaller, and freedom is finally in our grasp. Well except for curfew. And car insurance. And gas money. And repairs from learning what cars can and can not actually take from a new driver. Possibly a random grounding or two based on misunderstandings with law enforcement interpretations of speed "limits". No matter. Soon these annoyances will be behind us.

Check high school off the list.

College/trade school/full time jobs are here.

Finally, we have the freedom we deserve. No more curfew. No more teachers taking attendance.

We are finally in charge. It feels so good to be free. Come and go as we please.

Do whatever we want, whenever we want to. Except what's this? Rent? Utilities?

We even have to pay our own phone bill now??? No matter. Temporary setbacks. Soon we will be on to our careers!

THEN we are on easy street. Bills won't matter because we will be making more money than we can spend. Wait…what? Taxes and health insurance? Whatever. How much can those things really cost? Old people worry too much.

You know how the rest unfolds. Career, mortgage, family, toys, college for the kids, weddings for the same kids and the list goes on. Checking things off as we go.

We have achieved the ultimate in mobility.

We can go wherever we want now. Anywhere on the planet! If it fits the budget. And if we can both take vacation from work at the same time.

And if we have someone to watch the kids. Unlimited mobility within limits.

We have mastered the art of communication. We can say whatever we want. Almost.

We can say whatever we want if we choose our words carefully.

Even the slightest misinterpretation can end friendships, careers, etc. With our mastery comes a trap. We have become victims of overcommunication.

We make ourselves way too available and expect the same of others.

We have all the connection we could ask for. Spouse, children, coworkers, friends, acquaintances. Private time is a thing of the past. Don't even think about nap time.

We have busily and dutifully checked the tasks off the list. We have done everything according to societal expectations.

What's t next and how does this relate to recovery?

That task list mentality inevitably leaks into the brains and psyches of those seeking recovery.

A lifetime of programming seeps into our natural way of doing things. It does so because it works. At least we think it does.

The Triumvirate of Needs is no different in the lives of recovery seekers than it is in the lives of normal people.

We want mobility.

So often those seeking recovery lose mobility right from the start. Could be loss of a driver's license, could be loss of a vehicle, could be loss of courage to leave the house due to shame or embarrassment, could be loss of will due to tragedy or trauma.

We have earned and experienced mobility and lost it. We want it back.

We want communication.

One of the first things many of us experience in early recovery is loss of communication with friends and family.

They may choose to suspend communication because our actions were so egregious that they are struggling with understanding and forgiveness. They may be upset with themselves for not reaching out to help. They may avoid communication for no other reason than they don't know what to say.

We have experienced communication and lost it. We want it back.

We want connection.

The familiar faces and places we used to seek out for comfort are no longer comfortable. People may be polite, but they seem different. Some of that different feeling is real, some imagined.

Perception is reality though and it makes former connections feel broken. The feeling of not belonging to groups that formerly offered comfort and safety is devastating. We have experienced connection.

We want it back.

So, what do you think a person seeking recovery does once they decide that's what they truly want? We start attacking the task list ahead just like we did with the task list of life.

We work like crazy just to get through whatever it is we have to get through to get back to normal.

We need to go to physical therapy to get back to walking without help?? We work to physical and mental exhaustion and check every exercise off the list.

We need to go to counseling to help work through the loss of a loved one? We will go to a grief counseling specialist as well as a life coach so we can get back to normal as fast as possible.

We will go to every appointment and be there thirty minutes early and stay thirty minutes late. Every damn time.

We need to go to a twelve-step program?

We will go three times a day to show you how dedicated we are to getting better.

We will work through all twelve steps in record time and check them off the list as we go. We will share our story at every meeting so people can see our miraculous improvement and they can see it happen at top speed.

The harder we work, the faster we get through our task list and the better life will be. We just need to get this last thing done and we will be on easy street.

It is human nature to crave success.

We are driven to succeed as a species. It's hard wired in most of us. More often than not, hard work does pay off. Recovery, like life, is not a pile of big rocks that we are charged with smashing into smaller rocks and "call it good." There's more to it.

A lot more.

Working to physical exhaustion is rarely the best way to heal an injury.

Overloading on multi-discipline therapies doesn't allow us to absorb and process the information we are given.

Hurrying through step work for the sake of being "done" almost guarantees failure.

Recovery, like life, is a beautiful project to lean into. It deserves your effort and in turn, you deserve to bask in the glow of your hard-earned success.

Embrace that mobility you've worked so hard to regain. Sometimes a hangover free walk to the end of the street is just as beautiful as a trip to the Bahamas. Wave to your neighbors.

They will be happy to see you and even happier to see you doing well.

Utilize that communication skill you've refined to let people know how you are doing.

Explain the good AND the bad. Keep in mind that true communication is a two-way street.

Tell people how you are doing but don't forget to ask how they are doing. Listen to them. You will both gain from it. On your next walk to the end of the street, say hello to the neighbors instead of just waving.

Build on that mobility and communication and...

Embrace the connections you are making. You are becoming the very best version of yourself. You have earned the connections you are making.

Sharing your story helps people understand who you are and what makes you YOU.

People crave connection. Knowing someone's struggles and how they overcame them lends strength to others that may secretly need it. True connection is damn difficult to break. Maybe introduce yourself to your neighbors on your next walk. Even if they know your name, they may not know you. That would be a shame because you are definitely worth knowing.

You are working on a truly beautiful project. Like any beautiful project, others will naturally join in along the way.

Initially they may join purely out of curiosity and that's ok. They will stay because the project you are working on is just that good.

Eventually, if you manage things properly, there will be some very special people that carry on your work when you must leave.

Embrace your project. You deserve it.

38 NO MORE SECRET IDENTITY

October 2022

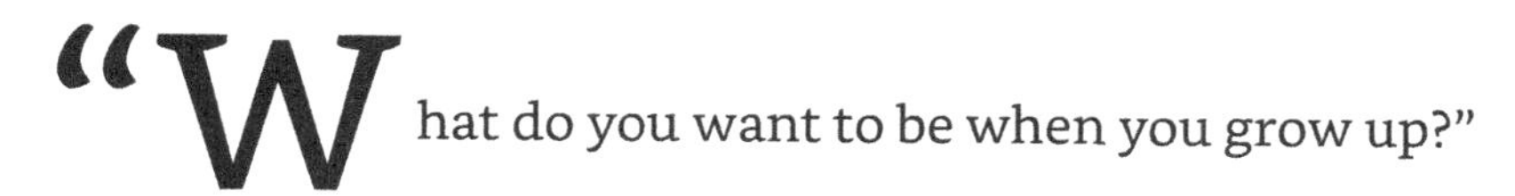

“What do you want to be when you grow up?”

“What are you going to do after high school?”

“Going to grad school after college?”

My responses, “Astronaut. Firefighter. Teacher. Police officer. President of the United States. Just like Mom and Dad.”

"Definitely going to college."

"Exploring my options but probably straight to an exclusive university to pursue a really impressive degree.”

“Definitely going to go on to get a master’s degree. Probably go for a PhD eventually. Really want to be competitive in the job market and rise to the top.”

Seriously...

How many times did I say any of those things knowing full well none of it was true, but more what I thought I was supposed to say?

I had a model rocket that got stuck in a tree the first time we fired it.

I was pretty good at soaking my little sister with a garden hose.

I taught my dog to climb a ladder (true story) and rode in a police car or two.

Still working on the President thing and trying daily to be more like Mom and Dad.

The actual extent of my childhood dreams.

I went to community college for a couple years then transferred to a four-year university to be with my high school sweetheart.

No associate degree from community college.

Quit the university to start a company with my Dad.

Lost my high school sweetheart.

I say some of this with a bit of tongue in cheek attitude. All truths but utilized for humoristic styling.

My life is not a miserable string of failures by any stretch, I promise.

Think about some of those events at the time they were happening though.

None of the things I told people I wanted to be when I grew up came to fruition.

I disliked community college, so I bailed on that simple exercise without so much as an associate degree or trade certificate.

I flat ass quit university because I hated school and saw an opportunity to do something that might make some money despite having no degree.

I found another pretty girl to chase and ended up marrying her.

Our marriage ended up about as successfully as my college career but that is a story for another book.

So why did I drag you through that lengthy setup? Sometimes a little self-deprecation combined with a dash of humor helps build relatability.

The moral of the story? How many identities did I claim or attest to pursue while failing or not even trying to achieve?

All of them.

Every single one.

Am I still working on being more like Mom and Dad? Of course.

Am I honestly working on a Presidential campaign? Yep.

I believe lightning can strike twice.

Most of those things were said as a wide-eyed youth that wanted to do everything, all the time.

Not becoming an astronaut, firefighter, teacher, or police officer were not true failures because they weren't actual pursuits.

Flubbing community college and solidly quitting university stung a bit later in life.

"How's school going, kid?"

"Umm... I am taking some time off to work on this business with Dad. I'll go back and finish up soon."

I kinda sorta meant it but not really. I HATED school. College specifically.

Dad made sure I understood that I had to go back in the fall and finish up my degree or else he would close the company.

I worked my ass off all summer to make sure we would be way too busy for me to go back.

Dad ended up selling the company 23 years later and I have yet to go back to school, so... I digress.

I was choosing my identity.

I was going to be the rebel that quit school and still made it big.

I wanted to be the "I sure showed them" guy. Possible insecurity issues much? Nah.

Most of us want to be like those that we admire and often emulate those that are best at the things we enjoy.

Fastest race car driver.
Most fearless yacht racer.
Richest businessperson.

The better we perform or are perceived to perform at the things we enjoy or deem important, the higher our "value" and the higher our perceived value, the more bulletproof our emotional armor.

At least that's what I told myself.

If everything is going according to prediction and plan, then my life is good. No questions asked.

What I saw: Business is booming. Beautiful family. Beautiful home in the right neighborhood.

All the fun toys. Invites to all the right parties from all the right people. This is what is meant by "living the dream", right?

We work to acquire status and standing. Each new milestone adds armor and gives us that next buzz.

Status and standing can be very addictive. They help shove the ugly stuff to the bottom. People don't ask questions on your way up. They certainly don't when you are at the top.

That top though.

It is a moving target, and the air gets awfully thin up there. Eventually there is no buzz. Everything is going so well.

Zero complaints.

It's everything we worked for, right?

The quiet time between buzzes is so very dangerous for some of us. It gives us a chance to look inside and realize that we do not like that view.

So we adjust. Let's change something. Add a project. Expand the business. Have a baby. Go back to school. Move to a new town. Take on an exciting new hobby.

Get people praising you again. Take a risk but get that fix.

Thought process: "People can't judge you when you are too busy to stop and chat. Most importantly, YOU can't judge you."

How many of you recognize the following exchange?

"Hey! How are you doing? Haven't chatted in forever!"

"Oh my gosh. Things are crazy. I'm just so busy! Working 12-hour days, running the kids to elite (insert sport here) camp, training for a half marathon because I am too busy to run a full one, running for the school board and getting ready for a trip to Europe.

You know, the norm. Just really busy. It's crazy but I love it. Let's get together soon!"

There's at least a chance we've all been on both sides of that conversation. Notice there was no mention of how the person is actually doing, just WHAT they are doing. "The armor of busy-ness." The air of, " Everything must be great. Look how busy he is!"

If there is no time to talk, there is definitely no time to answer any questions.

It works. Worked. For a while.

What happens when our identity starts to change? What happens when pieces of the armor start to fall away? There is a void that will need to be filled. There are vulnerabilities that need to be secured. This stage is a turning point where much can be learned.

Here is a dose of personal experience for demonstration purposes…

Lost my business.
Lost my marriage and in the process, my family.
Lost my home and lived in a barn with no facilities.
Lost friends.
Lost my spot racing sailboats and the camaraderie that accompanies it.
Lost the identities that I chose and had one I didn't choose assigned to me: hopeless drunk.

The unfortunate part of that assigned identity?

It was the most honest and accurate of all recent choices.

All the identities I created over a long period of time evaporated seemingly overnight. Vanished. Gone. What was I supposed to do? Embrace reality and ride "hopeless drunk" to the grave?

I almost chose that option as demonstrated by earlier chapters. Thankfully, I still had a core group of people that cared enough for the real me so that extreme choice didn't have to happen. Even with their help, it was close. Way too close.

Have you ever been there?

When my lie was outed it was devastating. I hurt lots of people.

Guess you could add "liar" to my new identity.

So, how do I get MY identity back?

What IS my identity?

Q. How do I get "me" back?

A. Brutal honesty and hard work.

Was I truly a hopeless lying drunk? At that moment I was. I needed to surround myself with people that were just like me so that I could fix me. Tear down the walls of the imaginary fortress and the useless, see-through armor and get to work.

It was amazing how simple the plan seemed in the schematic, but how difficult it was to implement.

Getting rid of the "drunk" was the first order of business. That allowed the "lying" piece to be removed from my title. Not long after those two labels fell away, "hopeless" did as well.

Good news! Gradually the "how are you doing?" question transitioned from an embarrassing reminder to a hope-building affirmation of truly being on the right track and sharing that with people who cared.

Things continued to get better as the work continued. I was able to hold a job and rebuild financially.

That meant no more homelessness or hopelessness. My identity was morphing from hopeless lying drunk to sober Derek.

That was so much better, right?

Absolutely emphatically, "Yes!!!!!"

And kind of "no."

It was SO easy to slip right into my new identity! It felt so much better than the previous one. It was almost as if it was mine from the beginning.

I was so relieved to be done with all the bad identities that I accepted and embraced the new one that was given to me.

The need for acceptance and connection overtook the need for a solidly built, core forged, self-created “me."

That was a choice fraught with danger. Potentially catastrophic.

I started to let resentment creep back into my thoughts. I resented being successful in my quest for recovery. I resented being known for getting sober. I was so many more things, wasn’t I? I was, but not at the moment. Not to others. Resentment breeds rebellion. Back to the identity drawing board.

Dammit. This cycle seems never ending...

Hold on though. That drawing board is closer than it’s ever been. You’ve been doing the work. You have been putting in the time. All the time and effort is about to be rewarded.

You have finally realized that YOU are in charge of your identity. This is a big win!

If your kiddos decide they want to enjoy more time with their friends or join band instead of trying to make the big leagues, have you failed?

If you decide that after dedicating fifteen years to golf that you want to race motorcycles, have you failed?

If you decide to throttle back on your career goals to spend more time with your significant other, have you failed?

Those answers are yours to determine and yours alone. You are the only one that gets to decide what life choices will do to your happiness. And your identity.

It is none of our business what other people think about us. None at all.

You have a massive, 100% responsibility to yourself to create and live your own identity.

It is your right, and it is one that you need to pursue and protect vigorously at all costs.

Life is a series of ups and downs. For everyone. You need to be prepared for both. It is critical to choose an identity that is true to your head and heart and focus on it.

It is important to continue personal growth as we work on this project of life. Triumph and tragedy will play a part in that growth. Do we have to let either of those conditions alter our core? Sometimes, but not always.

I had a core belief about recovery shattered as I was progressing toward my RCP certification.

Our instructor asked me for my definition of recovery.

That was an easy one. "Total abstinence from the abused drug of choice."

He pressed. "So a guy that drinks a fifth of whiskey a day and is a miserable human, puts in the time and work. He is now happy, healthy and has an occasional beer with the guys. By your definition, he is a failure."

My bumbling response? "Well…I mean…not so much a failure…"

The fifth of whiskey to the occasional beer guy was the opposite of failure because HE created his identity and was living it, happily and not at the expense of himself or his loved ones. He knew who he was. He worked hard to get to the point of being comfortable with himself again and was able to live life on life's terms. He no longer allowed others to assign him his identity. That is the pinnacle of satisfaction and inner peace.

Other people don't get to choose our identities anymore. They no longer get to assign values based on what they deem important from their outside perspective. Permission has been rescinded.

The flip side of that coin? We have to surrender our instinct to anoint others with identities as well. Put that mental judging apparatus away. For good. It makes things easier for everyone.

A long time ago, back in eighth grade, my English teacher profoundly impacted me.

She was a bit frustrated with the class and the lack of attention we were paying. She had us close our books then asked the class a question, "What was I just talking about?" Nobody had a satisfactory answer.

"Clearly you all heard me talking but were any of you LISTENING to what I was saying?"

That was awful to hear AND to listen to. She was one of my favorite teachers and not only did the class let her down, so did I. I could tell her feelings were hurt and I felt terrible.

Yes we all heard her but no, none of us were listening.

Hearing is a passive activity. We can look a person straight in the face, hear every word they say to us and not absorb a single thing they tried to impart. Why is this? Maybe we hear people talking but are more interested in hearing our own voice than theirs…?

Listening is an active pursuit. When we are listening, we are engaged with the other party. Comprehension and communication happens. Both parties are enriched by the exchange.

I've come to realize that sight and vision have an eerie correlation to hearing and listening.

We can see a person and their behavior and assign an identity or a judgment about them in an instant.

Our need for additional information stops because we have

gathered enough with that first glance.

It takes effort to look deeper and use true vision. The focused and detailed picture we create when we combine listening and vision is so much more accurate and complete.

We are going to talk more in-depth about sight versus vision in the next book.

Until then, embrace your positive new identity and self-image.

It looks great on you!

39 STOP AND TAKE THE SHOT

November 2022

There is a lot to take in from reading this book. From the ugly beginning to the beautiful ending, there is definitely something for everyone to chew on.

Or so I've been told.

One of the conditions I talked about in the very beginning was *Enthusiasm Blindness*. That blindness showed itself to me when something became obvious while I was proofreading these new chapters. I noticed how excited I was to reconnect with my current followers and to make new friends. There is something special that happens when you take a moment to reflect.

I am truly fortunate to have the best readers out there. I can honestly say that you are like family to me. We have been through so much together, yet you are still here, right by my side.

Time for a little give back to you.

We have walked a busy path to get to this point. Highs and lows. Humor and sadness. Heartbreak and triumph. There have been some easy reads that were mostly for fun and some that required deep and honest reflection. Some required homework and shifts in the way we treat people right down to the words we use.

I did a read through to see just how many things we would be doing if we incorporated everything asked of us in this book. It is a LOT.

Way too much to do all at once.
It is good stuff and going back through it has actually been super helpful for the guy that wrote all those words. My advice to myself was to pick one thing and work on it. Add another along the way when I am ready.

My advice to you is the same. Before you do that, let's just visit a bit.

Writing had never been a true pursuit prior to this book. It honestly started as a desperate act of a dying man. It ended up being a cathartic tool of a thawing soul.

It helped me process the things I had done and the things I needed to do to fix the damage I had caused.

Ironically, writing now fulfills the Triumvirate of Need we chatted about in Chapter 37. It allows me the mobility I desire which facilitates the connection I crave all while improving my communication.

It also forces me to be accountable for my own BS.

"Learn valuable lessons and share them with the world so they can avoid my mistakes...then forget about said lessons." It's not intentional. I am gifted with ADHD and love the distraction of the next shiny thing. I am the most Point A to Point B scatter brain you will ever meet.

Let me explain.

I was ecstatic when this book was finally published. I had finally found something I genuinely enjoy- Helping people through writing and making a difference makes me happy. Being able to make a living while helping people went from an impossible dream to a reachable goal. Reachable thanks to some incredibly well-timed help.

2021 was a whirlwind of a year. I accepted the position of EHS Director – North America for a firm in California. This position came with tons of travel. The year started by flying to Texas on New Year's Eve of 2020 and finally ended up back in Michigan for good on July 2nd, 2021.

There were a few trips home for short visits with Dad but the bulk of my time was spent anywhere from Oregon to Texas and all points in between. The reason I was home for good on July 2nd is hard to write about but it's part of my story, so it is necessary.

My Dad had been battling bladder cancer for a decade, give or take. It looked like he had it beat. He was feeling great again and all tests and scans were coming back clear.

Clear until fall of 2020.

"Probably nothing to worry about Derek but they found a tiny spot. It is cancerous but the doctor said we should be able to treat it with chemo. No big deal. Just keeping you informed per our agreement."

Dammit.

That was supposed to be his final scan because everything had been clear for so long.

The agreement Dad spoke of? It was a "full disclosure, no bullshitting me to keep me from worrying" agreement. Dad was Mr. Protective right to the end. I didn't mind that part; I just wanted all the data so I could choose what to worry about.

I asked him if I should turn down the job and take one here at home. There was lots of work and being closer would not be a terrible thing.

He looked me in the eye and said, "Absolutely not. You've committed to those folks, and they treat you well. Let's just see how things go and if I need you here, I promise I will ask."

I knew he wouldn't but that was our deal, so off I went. Dad and I chatted almost daily, anyway, now I would be listening a little more closely, that's all.

I worked a million hours on all kinds of cool projects while Dad worked a million hours on getting better.

Dad started chemo. *Again*. In the beginning he was doing ok with it for the most part. It did start to wear on him, and I could hear it in his voice. It was time for a flight home and a surprise birthday visit. I needed a break anyway and my "Dad batteries" needed a recharge.

"Hey Pop! How are things going? How are you feeling? Big plans for your birthday?"

"Hi Derek! Feeling kinda blah lately but plan on heading over to the cottage to get it opened for the summer. Looking forward to a change in scenery. Been feeling pretty shitty so thinking the lake might be good medicine. You coming home???"

"I was hoping to but we have a situation in California. Maybe we can celebrate a week or so after?"

"That sounds great. I'll probably feel better by then anyway."

Yep. That sealed it. I was flying home to see him. I spent MANY hours in airports on my way home. Just over 18 to be precise. Didn't matter. My head hit the pillow just before midnight on May 27th. Dad's birthday was the 28th and we were going to have cake.

I jumped out of bed super excited to see Dad. Bought a German chocolate cake (his favorite), some pickled bologna, cheese and crackers on the way. All things that were quintessential "Dad."

The cottage was about an hour away from my place, so I headed out early. I couldn't wait to see Dad and surprise him. It was such a gorgeous spring day with perfect sunshine. You could smell summer coming. I arrived at the cottage and no Dad. Hmm. Not like I was there at six in the morning. I gave him a quick call.

"Hey Dad! Happy birthday! You make it over to the cottage?"

"Hi Derek. Nah, not today. Feeling pretty shitty. Just going to lay low and take it easy today. Probably head over tomorrow. What are you up to?"

"Me? Not a hell of a lot. Just sitting in the driveway of the cottage."

"Aww. Shoot. I'm sorry. Let me get my ass in gear and head over."

"Don't you dare. I had an 18-hour day in airports and airplanes yesterday. I'll head home and do some laundry and take a nap. You just get rested up and I'll see you tomorrow."

"Sounds good. Thanks for coming home, Derek. I love you."

"I love you too, Dad. See you tomorrow."

Well, that wasn't good. I definitely wasn't expecting that.

We met the next day and it was so good to see him. He looked a little tired but still really good, all things considered. I did find out though just how bad the prognosis was, and it was not good news.

The cancer was not responding to treatment; it was spreading.

Dad was on a second type of chemo at this point, and it was really taking a toll on him. I needed to be home and a month later, I was.

I started going to his chemo treatments with him. We'd been

through everything else together, why not this?

During one of his five-hour treatments, I posed the following.

"Dad, I was thinking about giving writing a go. You know, as a full-time gig. What do you think?"

"If that's what you want to do, I think you should go for it. You've already proven you can do it, but do you think it will pay? *And would you go it alone again or would you hire some help like an agent or publisher or whatever?*"

He was grinning at me when he said that. Dad had a way about him. That was his way of saying, "I absolutely believe you can do it but maybe a little help would be ok, too..."

We walked through different scenarios and business plans. I had the capital saved up for something I could do on my own, just wasn't sure what.

Now I knew. Talking through how to go about it and how to set expectations was good distraction from what was being pumped into his veins.

We even ended up using our times in that room to get the bones of a collaborative book put together.

Dad would try two more experimental treatments that summer and fall.

The last one was slowing growth and spread and not making him feel like total garbage. It was an improvement and that was nice to see.

Things were going well enough that we were starting to plan on either racing my car again or starting to work on restoring his 1965 Mustang. Maybe both! It was so relieving to see him feeling better.

We had a great Christmas together.
Just short of a month later, Dad was gone.

January 24th, 2022 - A day that life forever changed.

Why did I take you through all of that?

Because sometimes it takes a major event to allow a major shift to happen. That was mine.

What does it have to do with stopping to take the shot?

Everything.

How many times was I too "busy" to drive over and see Dad?

How many times were Dad and I working on a project that I just wanted to complete instead of enjoying his time and embracing the project itself?

Too many times, for both.

I was finally in a position to start my own business again. Dad and I had a solid plan put together and better yet, we were ready to start our book together.

I figured since things were looking better, I would just work through winter then we could get started on the good stuff. I'll just go like hell for the next three or four months until everything is perfect and THEN we can get started.

Needless to say, things did not get perfect. Shoulda, woulda, coulda...

Dad passed at the end of January and I am finally writing this in November. It has taken that long to get my act even close to together.

I spent most of the winter and spring in various stages of guilt.

"Why didn't I go over and see Dad more?"

"Why was I so short with him when we were working on the race car?"

"Why (insert self-destructive question here)?"

I eventually discovered the answer. It was the simplest complex answer out there. SO simple and complex it could only be described as follows:

Life.

Life keeps us busy. Too busy? Sometimes, but not always. The further down the path of life we walk, the harder it is to become less busy. The more honest way to say that is the older we get, the less likely we are to modify priorities and change habits. That's the honest to goodness truth.

Remember the chapter you just read about being SO busy? Projected identity and self-assigned priorities. Neither are necessarily bad but all things in moderation, right?

If the conditions aren't perfect and the timing doesn't suit me, I'm just too busy.

At least I used to be. I was served a meal of "Stop It" soup and a "See?!?!" sandwich in October and it re-lit the fire to write.

One Sunday morning, I headed to Michigan's Upper Peninsula to meet with my new boss so we could map out the future writing plan and spend some time learning how to use my brand-new camera.

It may have also been to escape the chaos at my house as my furnace had finally expired. No big deal as I was *assured* it would be installed and *complete* on Monday.

Sunday was a perfect day. Went through writing projects as planned. Got to know my new boss even better and 100% solidify the fact that she was definitely the right person to herd this cat. We both learned some very cool things about photography that day as well. I never once felt foolish about my total lack of knowledge in the world of photography outside of my phone. Phone photography still sounds so silly to us Gen X types.

She was an excellent teacher. Time was not a factor. If there was a shot she wanted, we waited until people took their phone pics and moved on. I used to be of the mindset of, *"Oh well, too many people. I'll just take four or five real quick pics and get out of here. I'll just come back some other time."*

Then, I'd get home and look at the tiny few pics I did take be pissed at myself for not just waiting for three or four minutes to get the shot I really wanted.

Sunday was not only a day of discovering patience, but it was also a day of discovering different points of view.

We were shooting the exact same waterfalls from the exact same positions, but our pictures couldn't have been more different.

She could see the up-close stuff so much better than I could. I tried to zoom in like she did but couldn't frame the shot properly like hers. The lens I was using had the capability, but I didn't. I was clearly seeing the same waterfall as her but my vision for the shot was completely different. We will discuss that whole "sight versus vision" thing in the next book. *A literary device called foreshadowing...*

It was time to head out and I was packing up for the day when I got the text.

"Furnace not going to be in until Tuesday. Wednesday at the latest."

Not ideal, but I was not going to let that bit of info trash this amazing day. Time to make an adjustment. *(Kind of a big deal.)*

I decided to head to Marquette. My old college town. New camera, new skills, and new attitude. Marquette, Michigan is one of the most beautiful towns in the world. The leaves were changing color as fall approached and that added to the splendor.

Checked into my favorite hotel and sat down to look at pics taken earlier in the day.

Had a couple places I wanted to shoot on Monday then head home. I had to get back so I could work in a house with no furnace and things in complete disarray. I *really* needed to be there to supervise *nothing* being done.

Monday was glorious.

A beautiful sunny day. My Sugarloaf Mountain hike was spectacular as always as was the hike around Presque Isle Park.

I really *did* need to get back. I needed to be home to manage the *delayed* furnace project.

Oh, the "Tuesday no later than Wednesday" timeline turned into Thursday...moving on...

I wrote to my new boss and let her know about the ***unexpected extra delay in furnace installation***.

"*Awesome!* Enjoy your extended adventure and have fun taking lots of pics. Can't wait to see them!"

She *clearly* didn't understand the predicament I had so carefully explained.

I was in a gorgeous hotel room overlooking Lake Superior planning my hikes and travels in one of my favorite places in the world.

This was bad, dammit!

"Derek, this is why you chose the profession of writing. It doesn't have to be done at your desk at home. Go enjoy life. Yes, we have dates to hit but in between now and then: live a little."

Huh. *Again.*

I took her advice.

I enjoyed the hell out of my day Monday and extended my stay another two nights.

That enthusiastic, happy, genuinely excited advice allowed for some major breakthroughs.

I was able to acknowledge a broken heart I didn't realize I still had.

Marquette became MY town again instead of OUR town. Letting that go was necessary.

Next time I visit that town, my memories will be of my solo visit experiencing my new career path, not of someone that is no longer in my life.

Excitement, not sadness.

The final night of my stay was momentous and the inspiration for this chapter.

I'd spent all day exploring my town and its surrounding areas. I even did some scouting for the perfect place to take my sunset shot. I had everything planned. Perfectly. Until sunset.

I drove to my perfectly planned location only to find that the gate to the road around the park was closed. Didn't get the memo on that...

Hmm...Now what?

There was no way I could walk to my previously perfect location before the sun went down.

I'll just check the other side of the park.

Dammit! It is packed with people. What are they doing here on the west side of the park facing west out over the lake?

Now it really WAS impossible to get the shot I wanted. Come on people! Never mind that it is a 300+ acre park that is over two miles around.

“Oh great. Now look...Clouds," I thought. "The kind that makes some sunset pictures really spectacular," said no photographer ever.

This. Night. Is. Ruined!!!

Except it wasn’t. I made a very deliberate choice at that moment. I was going to do things the new way. I was going to walk to a random spot that I liked *then stop and take the shot.*

That’s exactly what I did.

I got to meet and help a mom that was taking her daughter’s senior pictures.

I got to walk down to a part of the beach that I’d never noticed before because I’d always walked the path in a counterclockwise direction as opposed to clockwise like that night.

The imperfect clouds, the imperfect setting sun and the imperfect spot all conspired against me and created some breathtaking views I almost missed.

I almost missed a perfect ending to the day because the variables weren’t aligning with my vision of perfect. I was almost happy enough to leave and try another time.

Valuable lesson learned, right? *Almost.*

I looked through the sunset pictures back in my room. So many cool shots.

THIS was my new way of living. Yep. I’m going whichever way the wind takes me. My new middle name is “Go With It."

Almost.

The next morning came early, and I was heading home. I knew which way was fastest and most direct. “Point A to Point B Man” at your service!!

Less than 8 hours earlier I had become "I'll Know I'm There When I Get There Man"...

I fueled up and pulled out of the way of the pumps. I grabbed my cellular camera phone and searched for waterfalls I hadn't seen before.

Found some! Wait...that detour would add three hours to my trip. I really need to get home to nothing being done on my heating situation.

I'll get the shot some other time. Need to get to Point B and time is a wasting.

"Bullshit!" I told myself. "I am going to see those waterfalls!" It turned out to be the right decision. I experienced some gorgeous waterfalls.

Got to meet some more awesome people. I was able to visit a town I'd never been to. I stopped and took the shot, and it was more than worth it.

Doing that reinforced the effort made with the sunset the night before.

I would be willing to bet that I have wasted more time beating myself up for missed shots or shots never taken than the time I would have spent just stopping.

We can't beat ourselves up for shots not taken. That doesn't help, it hurts.

What we can and should do instead is invest a little time into ourselves.

If you see an amazing sunrise on the way to work, stop and enjoy it. *Take the Shot.*

If the waves on the lake are extra beautiful one afternoon, stop and watch. *Take the Shot.*

If you see your neighbor out working in the yard, stop and help. *Give it a shot...*

None of those things take much time in the grand scheme of things, but the return on investment is very rewarding!

You will thank yourself later for the shots, I promise.

"Hey Dad...I just wanted to let you know I'm doing what we talked about. I'm writing full time now and yes; I found a professional to help me with it. I stopped and took the shot."

...MAN

10.01.19

Man. Man oh man.

That was a lot to go through. For both of us! Reading those chapters so I could edit them slightly and polish them a bit was hard. Looking back to see how bad things were was incredibly difficult. Totally worth it but difficult. And painful. And wonderful!

Alcoholics and addicts are NOT unintelligent people.

It may appear that way those not afflicted but nothing could be further from the truth. I spend many Saturday mornings sitting next to millionaires who take life one day at a time, hoping not to drink for 24 more hours.

That intelligence is a blessing and a curse.

So many of us have tasted success yet tossed it in the trash to have "just one more". Many of us are also problem solvers. We find success in solving problems for others while finding failure in our inability to fix our own.
I lost careers.

I lost friends. I lost my marriage.

In the end, I lost myself.

Figuratively and almost literally.

I created a self-fulfilling prophecy by continuing to drink and numbing reality. If it didn't hurt that bad, it must not be that bad.

It "wasn't that bad" all the way to the bottom. Reading through each of those chapters and going back to the journal

I've been keeping has been painful but therapeutic.

Each of us are definitely our own worst critics. It's amazing how much positive feedback we can receive yet still not believe it.
I don't know if normal people experience that as well or not. Definitely something to research before book number four.

The writing in the beginning was awful. Overly dramatic. Cheesy.
All over the place. Now I know why.

Three weeks into my journey to recovery, my friend Rich said I was just starting to thaw out. I didn't know what that meant until I re-read everything in preparation for this book.

He was being very kind at that point. Not sure how much thawing was happening as much as thrashing. I had a desperate need to prove to everyone that I wasn't that bad.

I had a desperate need to prove that to myself. If I was as bad as I thought I was, things were about to get a whole lot worse before they got better.

And they did. BUT because of the tools I gained in recovery and the support of friends and family, I was able to get through the rough stuff and start to see that things really could get better.

With my go-to coping mechanism poured down the drain, I stood there wondering what the heck to do next.

I learned that my reflex reactions to many situations were wrong.

My old thought process was to get the situation at hand addressed immediately, right or wrong, and get it behind me.

That freed my mind up to figure out the myriad other things I had messed up or was in the process of messing up. That thought process is so evident in my initial writings.

The chapters are in chronological order as is the healing process. I've always been told if I work hard and apply myself, I will succeed.

I still believe that but now I realize that things tend to happen when they are supposed to, not when I want them to.

I still get that manic feeling where my Enthusiasm Blindness takes over but it's not crippling anymore. Learning that enthusiasm can be good and bad has been an important step.

So as I stood there, facing an uncertain future with the wreckage of my past's icy hand on my shoulder, I committed to getting better.

Retraining my brain.

If it's not a life or death decision, give it a minute. Let it simmer but don't let it scald.

Ask yourself where the other person is coming from. Everyone is facing something or dealing with something that we don't know

about.
Not always easy to consider in the heat of the moment but the more we practice it, the easier it gets. Usually. (That was typed with a wink.)
Another lesson that had to be learned is we need to learn to like ourselves.
When I walked into AA that first time, I HATED myself.
Hated myself for failing at so many things. Hated myself for being weak.
Hated myself for becoming the person that I became.
Hated myself for not being able to solve the problem that was Derek Chowen.

A weak, stupid failure isn't easy to like, much less love. That subconscious self loathing is a powerful spell to break.

Talking with and more importantly, listening to people that were like me was incredibly powerful. Some of the most open and honest discussions happen inside those rooms.

The thrashing started to slow and the thawing started to happen.

New approaches to old situations were being learned. My mind, body and soul were adapting to the new reality and the new way. The need to maintain my social circles was intense in the beginning.

I loved being out and about and around people. I needed to affirm that I was still liked by others and that once they saw the effort I was putting in to making things right and getting well, things would go back to "normal". Soon that desire turned 180 degrees on me. I didn't want to see a soul.

I couldn't sit still in my own home but didn't dare go out.
Familiar places that used to be places of safety or comfort, were

no longer safe or comfortable. There were numerous factors that played into the 180 and the main one was my lie.

I live in a town of less than three thousand people. I've been here for almost 20 years.

The rumors were out long before I made my public confession. I didn't want to go to the grocery store for fear of seeing someone I knew.

Thank goodness for the early open times. But guess what? The feeling of terror of all eyes being judging eyes faded as well. Thawing, man.

So much continues to change. One of the Old Timers told me that the first two years of recovery are survival. Hang on kid. It's going to be worth it.

He was right. It still amazes me how things continue to change for the better.

This collection of thoughts gives you a peek into the mind of someone that transitioned from simply not drinking to LIVING life in long term recovery.

The writing is rough in the beginning, just as my life was. Practice helped both the writing and the living. People are fascinating.

Good people want people to succeed, no matter what. It is a refreshing place to be.

Surrounded by other former "professionals" and good people puts me in pretty darn good company! I hope this book helps everyone equally.

Understanding each other is the best medicine.

Stay sturdy.

The End

The Thawing Man

ABOUT DEREK

I was just about everything BUT a writer until I got sober. Business owner, stock broker, bank president, factory worker and bartender. Now I am an author.

I went from managing multi-million dollar portfolios to cleaning up puke from other drunks. Hitting the bottom allowed me to find my voice, and the confidence to use it.

Serving others is my calling and I am achieving that through writing and helping others. I opened a successful practice, GYBE Recovery Coaching Services. I am a certified Recovery Coach Professional. Private Coaching combined with writing and public speaking has allowed me the good fortune to reach thousands of people across the US and now, other continents. I've taken a step back from the private coaching to focus on other projects, but it's a component of my life and this book that we can't close the chapter on yet. One of the cool things about my new state of mind is that I can try this and see how it goes with no expectations. This book is outside of convention and self-published.

I'm probably writing this part wrong, too. But I'm doing it...and so can you. *Progress, not perfection.* ☺

Made in the USA
Monee, IL
07 July 2023

38404878R00144